PRACTICING THE PRESENCE OF PEOPLE

how we learn to love

MIKE MASON

best-selling author of The Mystery of Marriage

WaterBrook
PRES

PRACTICING THE PRESENCE OF PEOPLE
PUBLISHED BY WATERBROOK PRESS
12265 Oracle Boulevard, Suite 200
Colorado Springs, Colorado 80921

Trade Paperback ISBN 978-1-57856-265-7
eBook ISBN 978-0-307-56906-6

Published in the United States by WaterBrook Multnomah, an imprint of the Crown Publishing
Group, a division of Random House LLC, New York, a Penguin Random House Company.

WATERBROOK and its deer colophon are registered trademarks of Random House LLC.

Library of Congress Cataloging-in-Publication Data
Mason, Mike, 1952–
    Practicing the presence of people : how we learn to love / Mike
Mason.—1st ed.
      p.   cm.
    ISBN 1-57856-265-1
    1. Interpersonal relations—Religious aspects—Christianity
Meditations.   2. Love—Religious aspects—Christianity Meditations.
I. Title.
BV4597.52.M37   1999
241'.4—dc21   99-33834
                                                   CIP

Printed in the United States of America
2017

15 14

Dedicated to

Thelma Box

and to all the people of

Choices

"Changing the world
one heart at a time."

Contents

Contents

Contents

FRIENDSHIP _____ 221

Prologue

Twenty years ago I was sitting with my parents at the airport. I'd been home for a visit and now I was leaving. My life was a mess. I was an alcoholic and that was just the tip of the iceberg. The relationship with my parents was, to put it mildly, strained, and our visit had not gone well. Nevertheless, in those last few moments of saying our good-byes at the airport, something pure and good rose up inside me.

We were sitting on plastic chairs at a little round chrome table. I have no idea what we talked about. Normally I would have felt bored and agitated, counting the seconds until I could leave the company of these dull, vapid people with whom I had nothing in common except blood. Besides clock watching, I would normally have been girl watching, staring past my old mother and entertaining thoughts that had nothing to do with our stilted conversation.

Isn't this a good picture of modern man? Plagued by distractions, addictions, obsessions, never at home in his own skin, never truly connecting with others, never at one with present reality, and anxiously awaiting a plane going nowhere.

This occasion, however, turned out to be different. I don't know why; I don't know what prompted it. I wouldn't have known I had this in me. But suddenly all the distractions around me faded away, and I found myself absorbed in my mother and father, paying them the closest attention. It was just as if I were sitting across from a woman with whom I was falling in love. I remember feeling bathed in a kind of glow shining from their faces. Some well of wonder opened up, and I was touched inexplicably with a deep tenderness, a rush of gratitude for who these people were and for all they meant to me. Though the place was crawling with pretty girls, for once I was overwhelmed by something prettier and sweeter. Moreover I felt this as a movement in my will, as if this were not just a phenomenon that was happening to me, but something I was choosing.

For the first time in my life I was experiencing the conscious ability to enter fully into the here and now. This felt different from anything I had ever known, and I liked it. I loved the feeling of choosing to be real. I loved the sense of being fully there for my parents, of appreciating and loving them. Paying full attention to the people I was with gave me a taste of freedom that was like nothing else on earth. How did I know how to do this? Search me. But I wanted this feeling to last forever, and I determined to try to hold on to it.

Of course, like most grand resolutions, this one vanished almost immediately. A few minutes later I was on the plane, still savoring the unusual lightness in my heart, still basking in the glow of love. But all too soon the world of illusion came crashing back in, and I forgot all about my wonderful experience. In fact, ten years elapsed before anything like this happened to me again. And more years passed before I learned that the practice of the presence of people really is something I can keep happening in my life simply by choosing and cultivating it.

This book was inspired, as is obvious from its title, by Brother Lawrence's book *The Practice of the Presence of God*. For years I've had a love affair with this beautiful classic. Of all the devotional books I've read, this one seems to me the most practical. I've read it many times, and gradually its simple ideas about prayer have been woven into my heart. I like to think of my book as both a homage to Brother Lawrence and a kind of sequel to his work.

I love to pray. There's nothing I'd rather do. Socially I often feel awkward and insecure. But leave me alone in a room or beside a quiet lake, and I'm happy as a clam. A contemplative by nature, in years of solitude I've learned a good deal about what is known as *contemplative prayer*.

One day in contemplation there came to me the phrase *the practice of the presence of people*. And with it came this thought: *Why not take all that I've learned about knowing God through contemplative prayer and apply it to knowing people?* After all, since God is a person to whom we relate through prayer, shouldn't the principles of prayer also apply to knowing other persons made in His image?

Books originate in different ways: a persistent memory, an image, an opening sentence, a core idea. This book began with its title. For a long time that's all it was; I had no idea it would turn into a book. All I had was this compelling phrase *the practice of the presence of people*. Seven words, really just three words. For months I kept mulling this phrase over, pondering it and letting it ponder me.

While countless books have been written on the contemplation of God, I do not know of any book on the prayerful contemplation of people. Yet the more I pondered my phrase, the more deeply excited I became. In fact, so eager was I to experiment with this wonderful idea, I found myself spending more and more time with people!

Most amazing of all, I found that it works. By treating people the same way I treat God, I began to relax with them and enjoy them. Not only that, but the more I make my peace with people, the deeper grows my peace with God. The more I pay attention to people and connect with them, the richer grows my prayer life. The more I give myself to others, the more happy and fulfilled I feel.

In short, over the course of the year or so that I worked on this book, a miracle happened in my life: I, Mike Mason, lonely egoist, became a people person! I fell in love with love! From someone who had spent his life hiding from people in everything from books to nature to religion, I've become someone who sees God and touches reality most intimately through other people.

This is a story worth telling. There's too little love in our world, too little genuine friendship, too little real connectedness and community. I think there is great value in a book that addresses the question, *How do we learn to love?* For we are not born with love; it is something we must learn.

⌒

Learning to love is not a matter of following certain techniques, but of opening the heart. How the heart blossoms and opens up to love is a mystery. Accordingly, this is not a "how-to" book so much as a "who-to" book. For people, like God, simply are who they are. Loving them happens as we encounter this mystery. It comes through contemplation of who they are.

You'll sense what I mean if anyone close to you has died. In the physical absence of your loved one, what else is there to do but reflect, remember, contemplate? In the stillness, love grows deeper. Following the death of my mother, my father often said, "I only wish I could have loved her while she was still here the way I do now." This is the goal of contemplation: to love right now as we will in heaven.

Since mysteries are to be reflected upon, not explained, this is a book of reflections. It's a set of short meditations designed to be read slowly, devotionally. Each reflection is three or four pages in length, and these are loosely grouped into five categories or sections. The five categories might be compared to the fingers on a hand.

Think of the first section, titled "People," as the thumb. Other people often cut across our grain and oppose us, but without the opposable thumb a hand does not work well. How well are your relationships with people working? And how is your relationship with God? This chapter shows that the answer to these two questions is the same.

Section 2, titled "Self," can be represented by the index finger, the strongest and most dexterous. Do you realize you have a relationship with yourself? This chapter concerns the primary need to love yourself before you can love anyone else.

For the middle section, "Presence," consider how the middle finger rises above the others in stature. Scripture teaches, "Honor one another above yourselves" (Romans 12:10). We'll do this only as we realize that people are the presence of God on earth.

Section 4, "Practice," may be likened to the fourth finger, our weakest. As much as we may believe in love, how weak we are when it comes to actually practicing it!

The final section develops the theme of "Friendship." While the fifth finger may appear small, it's the one that most extends our reach. The result of practicing the presence of people is that rarest and most precious of spiritual fruit: rich, deep friendships.

Finally, there is one word that binds all these thoughts together: *love*. This is the palm of the hand: the flat, still pool in which love is cupped and held.

To contemplate God is to realize our oneness with Him in spirit. Similarly, the sign that we are practicing the presence of people is that we begin to feel one with them in spirit. We find ourselves seeing things about them that we never noticed before, understanding them from the inside out, tenderly identifying with their weaknesses, and marveling at their larger-than-lifeness. To be united to God, we must get over our fears and misconceptions about Him, coming to know Him as pure love and accepting His forgiveness so that no sin separates us. In the same way, being united to people means overcoming all our fears and judgments so that no sin or imperfection stains our fellowship.

Is this possible? Of course it is. It is called love, and "love covers over a multitude of sins" (1 Peter 4:8). Pondering this verse, I think of a gentleman taking off his coat and laying it over a mud puddle so that a beautiful lady in dainty shoes may walk across. In this parable, the gentleman is Jesus, the coat is His blood, the beautiful lady is you and I, and love is the bridge across which we walk into one another's arms.

PEOPLE

It is hardly necessary to remark that what kept Gibbie pure and honest
was the rarely developed, ever-active love of his kind.
The human face was the one attraction to him in the universe.
Gibbie knew no music except the voice of man and woman.
GEORGE MACDONALD

*A*t the time of my life when I fell in love with God, shopping malls were one of my favorite haunts. I had no money, so I didn't go to buy. I was unemployed and I needed something to do. Also, as a bachelor I needed to get out of my tiny apartment. So I went to malls to look at and to be with people.

Within two years I would have a wife, a job, money, and a church. But my first church, oddly enough, was the mall. That is, my first church was people. I might even say that simply being with people at the mall was my first real job and my first wife and family.

It was relaxing to sit there and take in the passing show. People looked different with glittering lights around them and high ceilings overhead. They appeared smaller, yet also, somehow, more dignified, as if they belonged in such palatial surroundings. The atmosphere was festive, ennobling. True, the looks on people's faces were less than noble or joyous as they rushed to and fro, struggled with their children, and mindlessly pursued their purchases. Nevertheless, to me they appeared beautiful. I felt that I had so much to learn from them just by looking. I felt that I had never really seen people in my life, and it was high time. It seemed I had a great deal of important work to do by just gazing, pondering, drinking in the mystery of people. There was something luxurious about being the only person, perhaps, in all this forest of materialism who was not driven by any material goal, who had no ulterior motive in being there except to be with people. There was something voluptuous about having, not only the time to do this, but also the inclination.

I'm well aware, of course, that myriad people, especially the old and the young, flock to malls merely to "hang out." But how many of them enjoy the ecstasy that I enjoyed? Because of my new belief in God, something had happened to my eyes and to my heart so that I was looking at the world in a brand-new way. Sights, sounds, and colors were more real and vibrant because suddenly I was seeing, as Gerard Manley Hopkins put it, "the freshness deep down things."

This was especially true when I looked at people. I was starving for the sight of people. I couldn't get enough of them. Sitting on a bench and watching the crowds was, to me, more lovely and restful than being beside a mountain stream. Peering closely into all these faces was like seeing my own face reflected in water. Without this looking, without this deep new seeing, how could people begin to understand one another? I wanted to understand. Something in the human form said, without words, everything that needed saying. Even these vacant and driven shoppers seemed to say it so eloquently, proclaiming with infinite expressiveness the ultimate of mysteries.

One time I saw a small robot being used as an advertising gimmick. He was about three feet high, rolled around the floor on invisible casters, and had a semispherical Plexiglas head bedizened with flashing lights like a pinball machine. This fellow had gathered quite a crowd around him. People were mesmerized, could hardly drag themselves away. The robot was remote-controlled by an operator who stood some fifty feet away, pushing buttons. Nobody was interested in this human. Nor was anyone intrigued that all around the mechanical wonder stood a crowd of flesh-and-blood wonders, each one inherently more complex and fascinating than any machine. It was almost as if we humans had forgotten how to be alive, and so we were praying to a computer to remind us. "O sweet little metal man," saic all those gawking eyes, "teach us, too, to be animate. Show us how to be thrilled with one another as we are with you."

How we do love our toys! Yet the real thing bores us to death. Wouldn't we have been better off that day forgetting the robot and spending our time marveling instead at each other? Isn't this what we secretly long to do? Isn't this why we all go shopping in the first place—not just to buy things, but to be with real people and to steal sidelong looks at them? So surreptitious is this work that we keep our intense curiosity hidden even from ourselves. And so there is no joy in it.

I find it fascinating that when I first fell in love with God, I fell in love with people, too. I fell in love with their faces, their eyes, their hands, the way they moved, how they are made. Those are *created* people, I kept thinking. I was not yet a Christian, so I had no elaborate theology for this. I did not know that people are made in the image of God. All I knew was that I liked going to malls to look at them.

This phase of being a mall rat passed. Soon my life moved on. Yet even today, twenty years later, I find myself returning to the revelation that was granted me in those early days of nascent faith. I don't hang around malls anymore. But whenever I do go shopping, I do not go merely to buy. For me the mall, or any public place, is too holy for that. However busy I am, however preoccupied, something stirs inside me in the presence of people, and I must put aside my list, my schedule, all my lovely plans, and take some time simply to gaze in wonder.

I am not saying this comes easily. On a good day, my store

purchases hold no charm compared to the people who sell them to me. But more often it requires an effort of will to pull myself back to what is really important: these living faces before me, these wondrous eyes, these radiant smiles, these serving hands. This, in part, is what I call the practice of the presence of people.

CHAPTER 1

Relationship

*P*aying attention to people is part of practicing their presence, but it is not all. It may begin this way, with an awakened, attentive gaze, but it must go much deeper than that. To see other people truly, one must look not from the outside but from the inside. That is, one must enter into relationships.

This is the part I'd been missing twenty years before with my mother and father in the airport. This is why my heightened awareness of them, though special at the time, remained but a fleeting experience. There was no true relationship to anchor the feeling of closeness. Love is a choice, and I had not yet chosen to enter into a love relationship with my parents. Like many children, I was still trying to disown them, still running away from home and so from myself.

The practice of the presence of people is not some spectator sport that can be done from the sidelines. We're not talking about people-watching, but about love. Love requires getting mixed up with people. We're going to spend a lot of our lives mixed up anyway. Why not do it together?

The view of people from inside healthy relationships is different from the view of the outsider. Even God wasn't content to sit alone in heaven. He became a man, entering the world and joining in the common life of His people. He wanted to get mixed up with us. Before ever inviting us to drink His blood, He took human blood into His own veins. Before asking us to eat His flesh, He lived among us, knowing hunger and eating our food.

The profound physicality of Jesus sets Him apart from other messiahs. The Apostles' Creed dwells on these physical details in a rapturous litany: "conceived…born…suffered…crucified…dead… buried…rose again…ascended…" The resurrection and the ascension of Christ were first and foremost physical events, which would have no meaning if He had not also done the commoner things—walking, talking, working, struggling, rubbing shoulders with real people.

God expressed His spirituality by entering into human relationships, by living and dying as one of us. He practiced the presence of people by becoming one Himself. So too each one of us must find a way to join the human race, casting off our separateness and throwing in our lot with others.

By worshiping an incarnate God, we learn to humble ourselves before one another. We sense that the quality of our spiritual life is no better than the quality of our human relationships, and that the way we connect with other people is an accurate picture of our connection with God. Jesus returned to heaven because we do not need Him to be physically present in order to experience the humanity of God. For He lives in you and in me. Most especially, He lives in *us:* wherever two or three are gathered.

One night in 1997, I drove with my family to a dark place in the country to view comet Hale-Bopp, the most impressive comet of my lifetime. As it happened, that same night there was a partial eclipse of the moon. So there we stood, on a deserted road, gazing up at the heavens in wonder. What a phenomenal display! Even so, I found myself looking at my family huddled around me and thinking that the real show was here on earth. We ourselves are the comets. We are the moon and the stars. We are the fireworks in a darkened universe.

To be in the presence of even the meanest, lowest, most repulsive specimen of humanity is still to be closer to God than when looking up into a starry sky or at a beautiful sunset. For we cannot really love a sunset; we can love only a person. God is love, and in coming to Him, we cannot escape coming through people. There is no separation between the spiritual and the social. The way we feel about people is the way we feel about God, and the way we treat people is the way we treat God.

Many of Jesus' parables illustrate this point. For example, in one story a landowner goes away on a journey, leaving his vineyard in the care of tenants. Yet whenever the owner sends servants to collect his dues, those servants are beaten and killed. Finally the owner sends his son, and he too is killed. Clearly the tenants would do exactly the same to the owner himself if they could get their hands on him.

The servants in this parable (Luke 20:9-16) are the prophets of God. But it is not only the prophets who are God's representatives on earth, it is also the poor, the sick, children, neighbors, our own families. Every person we meet is God's representative to us, looking to collect His dues. Are we paying up? Are we paying "the continuing debt to love" (Romans 13:8)? Or do we treat God's people with the civilized equivalent of killing and beating: ignoring them, isolating ourselves, sitting in silent judgment, rationalizing our love-lessness? "Whatever you did not do for one of the least of these," said Jesus, "you did not do for me"(Matthew 25:45).

If I harbor bitterness, envy, or anger toward any human being, don't I have these same underlying feelings toward God? And not only toward God but also toward all people, including myself. Every negative feeling I have toward another person is really a feeling about myself. To be angry with one person is to be angry with the world. If I want an accurate answer to the question, "How am I doing spiritually?" I need only turn my thoughts toward the one person in my life with whom I am having the most trouble. This person represents the place in my heart where peace with God is lacking.

There is nothing like another human being to confront us with our utter helplessness. In a sense, this is what people are for. We were not made to be independent but to be interdependent and to help each other. If we do not like to think about our true feelings toward other people, it's because this brings up our inadequacy. Good! God knows already that we are inadequate. Do we?

If only we could acknowledge our dependence on others—our basic need for love—surely the grip of all our personal problems would loosen. For is it not true that every problem has a damaged human relationship at its root? Sin might be defined as our attempt to solve all of our problems on our own, apart from relationship.

Now look at the person next to you and ask, "How much do I really want love?" No one can be close to God without also being close to people. A good friend of God will not be able to restrain his love for people. Do you love God? Look at the person beside you and you'll know.

CHAPTER 2

The Glory of the Lord

*P*eople reflect the presence of God in the world. The Lord has many other ways of being present; indeed He is everywhere. But nowhere is His presence nearer or more glorious than in human beings.

I remember clearly a time when this truth came home to me. I was attending an unusual four-day conference of Christians from all over the world. Pastors from many denominations were represented on the leadership team. Dozens of well-known speakers and musicians were present, and many of them shared their gifts. There was worship music, dance, informal testimony, preaching, and prayer. However, none of this was planned. There was no schedule, no agenda, for our sole purpose was to wait upon the Lord. This was to be a gathering led by the Holy Spirit, not by man. (Not that the Holy Spirit might not work powerfully through a planned format, but this was an attempt at something different.) The leaders felt that if they waited in simple, naked faith upon the Lord, He was sure to respond and give clear direction.

And so we waited. Every day, for as long as two hours at a time, two thousand Christians waited in patient silence. By the third day some significant things were happening. Many people appeared moved, excited. I should have enjoyed all this. Silent waiting upon the Lord was my own preferred style of prayer, and the idea of doing this with a large body of people from many traditions thrilled me. Nevertheless, I experienced nothing but a gnawing restlessness. I felt that I was in the wrong place, wasting my time.

I stayed only because I kept hoping for a breakthrough. This conference had been preceded by a massive buildup. Many people, and most of all the leaders, were expecting that "the glory of the Lord" would be revealed at this gathering. How or what this might look like, no one presumed to know. But all believed that God could not fail to respond to His people's heartfelt prayers.

On the final day of the conference, in the middle of one of the sessions, I got up and left to wander through the hallways of the enormous building. I was hoping to find someone to talk to about my frustration.

All at once I saw a familiar face, a neighbor of mine, Shirley Gemmell. For several years I'd been friends with Shirley's husband, Bob, and even dedicated a book to him. But I did not know Shirley well, nor did she know me. In those days I knew hardly anyone, and hardly anyone knew me. Bob had had to work hard to befriend me, for I was an awkward person, insecure, distant, intimidating. The range of topics on which I could comfortably converse was narrow.

So, although Shirley was warm and friendly, she might as well have lived on the moon for all I cared.

Yet as I passed this woman in the hallway, without thinking I said to her, "Shirley, I love you."

What?! Seldom had I spoken these words to anyone except my immediate family. Yet to say them now, spontaneously, felt perfectly natural. Something about Shirley's face was soft and inviting. I would even say her face was shining, glowing in a relaxed, ordinary way. It seemed the most normal thing in the world to tell her from my heart, "I love you."

At the same time, it struck me as an extraordinary miracle. Afterward I pondered this incident for days, weeks, months. It was the one thing I took away from that conference. I think now that it may be the most important thing I'll take away from life itself.

Following the conference, I happened to talk to one of the leaders, a man I deeply respect. I asked him whether the one great expectation of the conference had been fulfilled. Had the glory of the Lord indeed been manifest?

Somewhat sadly, this man shook his head. Many special things had happened, he said. But no, as far as he could tell, the glory of the Lord had not appeared.

I then told him cautiously of my experience with Shirley Gemmell in the hallway on the final day. Though I did not use the phrase *the glory of the Lord,* inside I felt just as excited as if I had seen a vision of Jesus. Yet as I told this story, I saw that it did not hold the same meaning for my friend as it did for me. I sensed my words falling to the ground as I spoke. And so I concluded that in our day *the glory of the Lord* may be a subjective rather than an objective phenomenon. One person sees it one way, another experiences something else. It comes down to a matter of perspective.

I don't believe this anymore. I now know that what I saw that day on Shirley's face *was* the glory of the Lord. In the Old Testament, God's glory took external forms, such as the pillars of cloud and of fire that led the Israelites through the desert. Still today there are reports of such phenomena. In the New Testament, however, a "surpassing glory" was revealed, a glory so much greater than smoke or fire that it inspired Paul to write, "What was glorious has no glory now in comparison with the surpassing glory" (2 Corinthians 3:10).

What is this greater glory? I believe it is the light of God shining from the faces of His people. It is what we see in one another when we love.

What happened to me that day with Shirley was nothing short of a revelation of God's love. In one instant the Lord showed me what life is all about: It's about seeing the image of God in people and loving them with a pure love.

While this mystery had been shown to me many times before, each time I had dismissed or forgotten it, as though it weren't enough. Now I saw it for what it was. This revelation was imprinted on my heart in such a way that I began to choose it consciously. After this the pattern of my life became a deliberate, gradual responding to the glory of God's love as revealed in human faces.

CHAPTER 3

Christ in You

*B*ecoming a Christian begins with recognizing God in one human being, Jesus Christ, and goes on to the recognition of God's image in every person. Having seen in Jesus God's glory in human form, we now know what (or rather *who*) to look for in all God's people. As Jesus said, "I have given them the glory that you gave me" (John 17:22).

I once wrote a book on visions of heaven. My research involved talking to a number of people who regularly have spectacular visions. Getting to know these people, I grew jealous. I began to pray that the Lord would grant me such experiences, and eventually He answered me in a surprising way. He said, "Why should I give you visions of heaven when you cannot see what is right in front of your eyes? How can you see Jesus in heaven when you cannot even see your own neighbor on earth?"

This answer both startled and shamed me. I've been thinking about it ever since. It's true: There's a brightness in the human face that is almost too bright for human eyes. It seems we can look at each other only so long before we must turn away. Perhaps we are too used to being blind, too accustomed to living in the dark. If we could really see what is right in front of our eyes, we'd see the invisible, too.

"Do you not know," wrote Paul, "that your body is a temple of the Holy Spirit?" (1 Corinthians 6:19). In the Old Testament God's temple was a building. Then, as now, the world was full of people who could have displayed God's presence much more radiantly than any temple of wood and stone. But people were not ready to carry the divine flame, nor even to look upon it. When Moses descended from the mountain after meeting with God, his face shone. But "the Israelites could not look steadily at the face of Moses because of its glory" (2 Corinthians 3:7). Even today a veil hides this glory from all unbelievers, for "only in Christ is it taken away" (v. 14). As Paul declares in the climax to this passage, "And we, who with unveiled faces all reflect the Lord's glory, are being transformed into his likeness with ever-increasing glory" (v. 18).

Just before Lazarus was raised from the dead, Jesus told Lazarus's sisters, "Did I not tell you that if you believed, you would see the glory of God?" (John 11:40). What was it that Mary and Martha saw that day? More than a miracle. The miracle happened inside the tomb, in darkness. There was no earthquake, no appearance of angels, nothing supernatural to see. What, then, did Mary and Martha see?

They saw a human being, a man, walking toward them, and that man was the brother they loved. Is it possible that this, as much as the miracle of resuscitation, was what Jesus meant by "the glory of God"? Indeed I believe this is the heart of the gospel: seeing and being the glory of God in human form. This is what Paul called "the word of God in its fullness…this mystery, which is Christ in you, the hope of glory" (Colossians 1:25-27).

Lazarus was not resurrected. He was not able to walk through walls as the resurrected Jesus was. Lazarus, rather, was simply restored to ordinary life. Yet how the veil was suddenly ripped from that ordinary life and its glory revealed! Imagine the reunion that must have taken place among the two dear sisters and their brother! Just before this, Scripture records that "Jesus wept." But imagine the tears of joy and laughter as this precious family, freshly bathed in the glory of God, embraced and celebrated! No doubt they were all filled with a wondrous new revelation of the mystery of human life, and henceforth they would all love each other more deeply than ever.

As Lazarus stood outside his own tomb, bandaged and blinking in the light of day, Jesus said, "Take off the grave clothes and let him go" (John 11:44). But have not all of us been "raised with Christ" (Colossians 3:1)? It's time to take the graveclothes off the church and let her go. It's time to practice the presence of people.

CHAPTER 4

God's Prayer Life

*M*y friend Bob Kirk is a pastor. He once told me that there was one message he wished he could convey to people in his church, especially to leaders. Unfortunately he found that this message was almost impossible to communicate. The people who needed most to hear it, Bob said, seemed unable to grasp it. Having tried again and again to say what was burning in his heart, Bob had all but given up. He told me he had concluded that the message was inexpressible.

My curiosity piqued, I begged him, "Please, can you try expressing it for me right now?"

Bob thought for a while and then answered: "I'd like to tell the church to let people be human. I'd like them to learn to enjoy humanity, both their own and others'. To enjoy and to accept humanity, with all its warts and weaknesses, without pulling away in fear and judgment—this is the one thing the church doesn't know. Most churches, I think, are frightened of human beings."

If you are frightened of other people, it may be because you are frightened of yourself, of your own humanity. Everything in creation seems better organized than we are. All around us we see nature obeying immutable laws, while we alone create our own laws, for we alone have free will. The ocean waves roll into shore with a good deal of orderliness, and the stars wheel predictably in their courses. Meanwhile, we're trying to decide what to wear to the party.

According to fiction writer Jim Harrison, "Part of the struggle of the novelist is to convince the reader that the nature of character is deeply idiosyncratic to a point just short of chaos, that the final mystery is the nature of personality."[1]

Letting characters be human is not just the novelist's work, but everyone's. It is God's own work as He creatively challenges us to be our true selves, even when the reality of who we are seems scary and bewildering and flies in the face of social convention. Like it or not, real life is not lived on some quiet millpond, but out on the open ocean in all kinds of weather. What would it take to convince ourselves that it is right and good for our characters to be formed in this wild, peculiar, haphazard fashion?

"In creative writing courses," says novelist Carol Shields, "one of the first things you learn is to keep your characters consistent. This is bad advice, because human beings are not consistent. In fact the very moments that are most interesting are the moments in which people act inconsistently, out of character, when they suddenly leap up and become larger than they were."[2]

Are you frightened of inhabiting your peculiar niche "just short of chaos"? One thing is sure: If you deny the bizarre and the grotesque in yourself, you'll never accept it in others. To the extent that you shrink from the disorderliness of people, love will scare the daylights out of you.

Of all the books in the Bible, probably Psalms is the most frequently read. These sacred poems portray a vision of humanity so large and deep that every mood of the heart is covered, every foible, every pettiness, as well as the grander and nobler sentiments. The psalms tell it like it is; they let it all hang out. In the process, they teach us that God hungers for real people. In fact, like the novelist, creating real characters is the work that absorbs God's grandest energies night and day.

Halfway through the writing of this book, I saw the dazzling irony of my title, *Practicing the Presence of People*. What I saw is that God has a devotional life too, and that just as our prayer life consists of practicing His presence, so His prayer life consists of practicing our presence. God loves to keep us as the apple of His eye, and it's a good thing He does, for if He ever ceased—even for a moment—you and I would vanish like smoke.

You and I do vanish from each other's lives to the extent that we fail to look upon one another with the fearlessness of unconditional love. To practice the presence of people is to enter into the prayer life of God by seeing people His way.

CHAPTER 5

A Poor Reflection

Recently my friend Bill Volkman told me, "I haven't seen much in my life. I haven't really seen my children or my grandchildren. I haven't seen their faces, their smiles. I guess I've had my eyes open all this time, because I haven't been bumping into any walls, but in my seventy-two years there's not much that I've really seen. Only now is my vision starting to clear, a little more each day. How marvelous to be able to see people!"

Have you, too, noticed how hard it is to see people clearly? It is one thing to look, but it is quite another to see, and still another to hold what one sees in focus in the heart. Even when people are motionless, still they appear to be moving slightly, swimming across the field of vision. Their image jiggles, blurs, refuses to hold still. It's like trying to examine the moon through binoculars without a tripod. You wish the thing would stop dancing around.

Of this phenomenon Paul wrote, "Now we see but a poor reflection as in a mirror; then we shall see face to face" (1 Corinthians 13:12). Wasn't Paul talking here about God? Maybe. But the context—all about the importance of loving one another—suggests that he may have been thinking too of the difficulty of seeing people.

There are many reasons for this difficulty. One is that people are literally larger and more mysterious than anything one can take in. The image of God is not something to be photographed, pinned down, or understood with the mind.

Another difficulty is that people really are moving around—not just on their legs but in their souls. People are less like stationary stones than like rivers, always flowing, changing from moment to moment. The best way to see people is to jump into the river with them and form relationships. Then, at least, we are moving together. This is what relationships *are:* people in motion together. Only as we move together does it become possible to find stillness.

I remember seeing this clearly at a wedding dance. Feeling melancholic, I sat for a long time alone on the sidelines. I tried to tell myself that I was enjoying just watching, but I knew I wasn't. Not until I actually got up and joined the dance was I able to see what was going on. Suddenly I felt one with the party. How vibrant and beautiful everyone looked! It came as a great eyeopener that my eyes actually worked better while I was bouncing up and down. I could see life more clearly as a participant than as an observer.

Another difficulty in seeing people clearly is darkness. The fallen world is a dark place, and we ourselves are bleary-eyed, like myopics in need of glasses. Hence people appear like shades or ghosts floating in a darkling mist, not quite solid, not quite there. Novelist Stephen Lawhead describes a character who breaks into the Celtic *Other-*

world where everything appears more vibrant and real. Upon returning to this world, he is shocked at the appearance of people here:
"Their features were coarser, their bodies smaller and more ungainly.
They appeared slighter, less physically present somehow. There was a
peculiar ghostlike quality to them, as if they clung to corporeal existence by the slenderest of threads."[3]

Doesn't this describe something of the way we actually experience others? If people appear skewed, it is because fallen beings really
are this way, diminished from glory to a shadow of our former selves.
Even so, in the midst of the wreckage, it is possible to catch glimpses
of the ancient fire, and a flicker too of future glory.

People are difficult to see, finally, because we are at least two
kinds of being rolled into one. Paul speaks of the "old self" (Romans
6:6) and of the "new creation" in Christ (2 Corinthians 5:17). Believers are no longer mere *homo sapiens* (rational man) but are remade
into *homo fidens* (believing man). Through faith we are literally
changed into a new species.

To practice the presence of people is to choose deliberately to
focus on the new creature rather than the old, to see the light in
people rather than the darkness. Everyone has a light side and a dark
side, a true self and a shadow self. The shadow self, just like a shadow,
will cling to us for all of our earthly lives, but it has no real substance.
The only substance it has is what we and others create by fearing and
indulging it. When we eat an apple, we want a real apple, not the
shadow of an apple. Yet many people spend their lives walking
around inside their shadow selves, letting their dark side dominate
and never coming out into the light.

In the beginning God separated the light from the darkness, and so must we. We must help one another to see and to walk in the light. We do not disregard the darkness, but we do relegate it to the fringes of a person's being, not the center. In this way the darkness becomes only a frame for the true picture.

CHAPTER 6

Believing in People

We gain access to heaven by believing in God through Jesus Christ. Similarly, we gain access to earth by believing in people, also through Jesus Christ.

Believing in God is important; believing in people is also important. This is James's point in arguing that "faith without deeds is dead" (2:26). "You believe that there is one God. Good! Even the demons believe that—and shudder" (2:19). To complete your faith, you must put it to work in the real world, by believing not only in God but in people.

Perhaps as a Christian you feel quite pleased with yourself for believing in God. But how much do you believe in your brother the alcoholic? How much do you believe in your son who is on drugs, or in your pregnant, unwed daughter? Do you believe in your neighbor with whom you think you have nothing in common? Do you believe in prisoners, in the mentally ill, in hopeless cases? Or do you write such people off, believing only in those who are just like you?

To believe in God is to believe not only that He is real, but that He is good. Believing in people is similar. Admittedly, it is a bigger stretch to believe in people than to believe in God, because God really is good, while people are not. "The heart is deceitful above all things and beyond cure" (Jeremiah 17:9). Jesus said even more bluntly, "No one is good—except God alone" (Mark 10:18). In the face of what theologians call the "doctrine of total depravity," isn't it a lie to believe that people are good?

No, because the fact remains that people were created good. To believe in human goodness is to recall God's original plan. It is to focus on His original intent for our lives. This is belief, not present fact. We're talking about an act of prophetic faith. Believing that people are good will not make them so, but it will issue a powerful invitation. By having faith in people, we dramatically increase the odds that they will actually behave well and grow in virtue. This is not naive positive thinking, but a matter of practicality. It's better to believe than not to. Faith works.

In order to believe in people we must make a decision to know only the good in them. If our eyes are open, we'll see the evil, too, but we must decide to know only the good. After all, only the good can truly be known. Good reveals, evil conceals. The evil in people is what keeps us from knowing them. To know them, we must look to the good.

By looking at people with the eyes of faith—past all the masks, the games, the lies—we pierce through to the truth of the person whom God created. God did not create anyone to be a failure, a thief, a drunk, a bore. This is not who people are. Who, then, are they?

Faith answers the question of who we are. The more we try to grasp this riddle intellectually, the less sense it will make. Rational knowledge has to do with what and why, not who. The knowing mind is forever sorting through all the available facts, the evil along with the good, weighing this against that, seeking to determine the good by deduction. But the good cannot be known this way, for the good is not a what or a why, but a who. The great question in life is not, "What should I do?" or "Why?" but rather, "Who do I know?"

Job found this out. After thirty-odd tortuous chapters of what-why questions from Job and his friends, the Lord finally answered with some questions of His own: "Who cuts a channel for the torrents of rain?... Who fathers the drops of dew?... Who has the wisdom to count the clouds?... Who has a claim against me that I must pay?" (38:25,28,37; 41:11).

To know who, we must give up the pursuit of knowledge and simply believe. Only then do we gain the power to counter evil, not by seeking to know or to understand it, but rather by knowing and doing good. In the pursuit of good, evil is thrust aside as surely as the headlights of a car push darkness out of its way. Darkness still surrounds the car on all sides, but enough of the road is illuminated to make a clear path ahead.

The Beatitudes speak of those who travel in darkness but have abandoned the need to know anything about it. The poor in spirit, the pure in heart, the merciful, the meek—such souls are no longer asking, "Why does God permit evil?" or, "If God didn't want us to eat from that rotten tree, why did He create it in the first place?" No, these faithful ones are not preoccupied with evil, for they have "seen a great light" (Isaiah 9:2). So overwhelmed are they by pure goodness that they do not know anything anymore—they only know Who.

Like Paul they can say, "I know whom I have believed, and am convinced that he is able to guard what I have entrusted to him for that day" (2 Timothy 1:12).

Faith, whether in God or in people, can only happen in utter humility. It implies a willingness to have neither questions nor answers, only an open ear and a clear eye. It means entering the larger-than-life presence of others and letting them teach you who they are. It means being content to be at sea, often just beyond your depth. It means expecting to be moved in surprising ways.

If you feel bored or trapped in your relationships, it may be because you're trying to relate out of your mind rather than your heart. Practicing the presence of people requires listening to the heart, which speaks only through relationships. The mind can function more or less on its own in a closed system of self-centered thought. But the heart requires bonding with others.

Jesus said, "Do not let your hearts be troubled. Trust in God; trust also in me" (John 14:1). He might have gone on to say, "You trust in Me; trust also in other people." Perhaps our motto should be, "Let go and let people." Some of the blind have seeing-eye dogs. They have to let go and let dog. But we all need seeing-eye people in our lives, people we trust enough to guide us into truths we could never discover on our own.

Trust must be built. Like faith in God, faith in people matures over time, through experiences both pleasant and unpleasant. Over and over we must make the decision to believe, not expecting to have one big experience that will suddenly purge us of all uncertainty, but rather taking the small daily steps of trust that lead by gentle increments into the depths of intimacy.

CHAPTER 7

Look in the Mirror

D o you realize that what you see in others is only what is in yourself? Think of other people as a mirror: What do you see when you look into the mirror of humanity? What is reflected back to you? Is your mirror cloudy or clear? If you recognize God in your own life, you'll see Him everywhere. If you love yourself, you'll love everyone. You may think you love yourself, but the extent to which this is so will be accurately reflected in your view of others. How happy you are is directly related to how many people you can embrace with love. The more the merrier!

The mirror of flesh and blood is the test of true love for God. A flat silver mirror gives one sort of reflection; peering into a clear mountain lake provides a different reflection—not so distinct as glass, yet deeper, more vibrant. But the best mirror of all is other people.

Do you, like me, tend to resent God for remaining invisible? If only He would show Himself, we think, then we'd know where we are. Like Job we complain, "He is not a man like me that I might answer him" (9:32). Meanwhile, the world is full of people, fully visible, radically alive, talking up a storm, gesturing like crazy, all clamoring for attention—as if God Himself were standing on a soap-box and yelling out to the heedless crowds passing Him by, "Over here! I'm over here! Can't you see Me?" Isn't our blindness to the actual presence of God in this world so preposterous as to be comical?

If Jesus Christ were still on earth in the flesh, we'd probably say to Him, exactly as Philip did, "Lord, show us the Father and that will be enough for us" (John 14:8). But would it really be enough? If the Father Himself were standing right in front of us, wouldn't we likely say, "Show us something else!" The question is not whether God is real, but whether we ourselves can ever trust Him enough to be sat-isfied with Him. Our chronic state of gnawing restlessness gives us away. If we're unhappy now, after Jesus has already come and suf-fered and died for us, then we'll be unhappy no matter what He does. He could stand on His head and wiggle His toes on top of a Christmas tree for all the difference it would make.

Does God seem distant or absent? It may be because you have chosen to distance yourself from His people. You have good reasons for this: disillusionment, distrust, childhood wounds, a long history of real hurts and failures. Still, if you want to travel out of your lone-liness into the country of love, there is only one way, and that is by making real contact with other people.

"If you are offering your gift at the altar," taught Jesus, "and there remember that your brother has something against you...first go and be reconciled to your brother; then come and offer your gift" (Matthew 5:23-24). How fitting that intimacy with God deepens only as we humble ourselves before fellow humans. The precincts of holiness are crowded with people. We must make our peace first with Jesus and then with everyone.

Religious types are always asking, "What is God saying?" But what are people saying? Once I confronted a well-known Christian leader with his alcoholism. He wouldn't listen. He said that before he'd believe me, he'd have to hear it from God. Meanwhile his wife was telling him how much she hated his drinking; his children were telling him; other friends were telling him; and I was telling him. But no, he was waiting to hear it from God.

Relationships—even bad ones—speak loudly and clearly. Listen to them. They will tell you the truth about yourself, while on your own you will certainly miss it. What are the people in your life saying? What is your neighbor saying? What are you saying? Do you know? When you find out, you may discover that God is saying virtually the same.

"You want to hear My voice," says the Lord, "but you do not listen to the voices of My people.

"You want to see My face, but you will not look into the eyes of My people.

"You say you want to know Me, but you do not want to know My people.

"You want to be healed, and you want to lay your hands on others to bestow healing in My name, and yet you will not enfold your brother in a heartfelt embrace."

John summed this up when he wrote, "Anyone who does not love his brother, whom he has seen, cannot love God, whom he has not seen.... Whoever loves God must also love his brother" (1 John 4:20-21).

CHAPTER 8

Permission to Love

W hy does it seem so hard to love? Why does the real thing so
often elude us? Why don't we just claim this treasure and
enjoy it?

One reason is that we do not really believe love is permitted.
Love is so beautiful, so safe and pure and good, that we cannot bring
ourselves to trust that it is allowed to us in a world so dark and full of
pain. A little taste of love here and there—yes, that is fine. That
much we'll accept. But to make love the central purpose of our lives,
to build everything else around it to the point of filling entire days,
hour after hour, with nothing but love—why, such a life would be
unthinkably idealistic. It would be just plain silly.

Shortly after meeting my wife-to-be, I was overcome with panic
and confusion. I knew I loved her, but love implied marriage and I
wasn't ready for that. Indeed I was happy being single and convinced
I had a call to celibacy. I was seriously considering a monastic life.

In my turmoil I sought counsel from a former teacher, a Jesuit
priest. Laying the whole situation before him, I hoped and expected
that he, a celibate himself, would confirm my monastic vocation and

encourage me in that direction. I wanted him to say, "My son, there is no temptation greater or more dangerous than a woman. Flee from her with your life!"

But instead this kindly old man regarded me tenderly and asked, "Do you love her?"

My jaw dropped and I gawked at him. Perhaps this fellow was not as wise as I had thought. After a long pause, I answered him with a question: "Of course I love her—but what does that have to do with it?"

These were my very words. Recalling them now, I can hardly believe my naiveté. Still, isn't this the one basic question we all have?

What does love have to do with anything?

Don't we have other business to attend to, other matters more pressing? What does love have to do with finances, with meeting deadlines, with going to the dentist or to the unemployment office? The world is not *about* love, for heaven's sake! Love has its place, but it mustn't be allowed to run our lives. Oh no! If we must have love, then let it be a little fling here and there, or else something pragmatic, hard working, goal-oriented. The idea that love might actually be fun, relaxing, renewing, exhilarating, and that we might enjoy such love not only now and then but as a way of life—this is too much.

In short, it is not okay for us to let love be altogether wonderful. We hedge it round with bleak practicalities. We mix it with everything else: duty, money, power, piety. Love for its own sake, for the pure, delicious joy of it, might be allowed us in small doses, but not as a steady diet.

What if we uncorked the bottle and let love loose in our lives? If love pure and simple were ever permitted to rule the world—why, think what would happen!

Exactly.

This is the problem. Love, if allowed free rein, would overthrow the world system as we know it. Nothing could stand in its way. Everything would topple like a house of cards: stock markets, governments, the Mafia, shopping malls, banks, libraries, our jobs, and on and on.

Isn't this what we're all afraid of? Aren't we terrified of our little world caving in around us? But the destruction of the world by love is the goal of the gospel. The gospel is a license to love. It is a unilateral declaration that from now on there is only one law: the law of love. All other laws, all other organizing principles, all other systems of morality have been superseded. We no longer need to live for anything but pure love. The gospel grants us full permission to devote ourselves unashamedly to this foolishness. No longer is there the slightest justification for pursuing any other goals except these two: Love God and your neighbor.

If we like, we can sit around endlessly speculating on the meaning of love. But why not just get on with it? Why not simply obey the gospel and "live a life of love" (Ephesians 5:2)?

My friend Mike Tronson went through a long period of unemployment. During this time he was plagued with insecurity, doubts, questions. What was he to do with all the time on his hands? Without working, how was he to justify his existence?

One Sunday his pastor happened to ask in the sermon, "When you're praying, do you ever just pause and ask God to speak to you?"

A few days later Mike was in his garden, praying. Once again his thoughts were taken up with the difficulties of unemployment. But recalling his pastor's comment, Mike paused and asked God to speak to him. Immediately the Lord said, "This is a time to focus on your wife and children. Learn to love them more deeply. Work is of very little importance to Me. What's important to Me is people."

This thought washed over Mike with a wave of freshness and relief. God had given him a job! Instead of feeling anxious about not having work, now Mike was free to focus on the most important work of all. He had just been given permission to love.

CHAPTER 9

The Answer
to All Problems

Often what keeps us from loving is a sense of being swamped by our own problems. But listen: The practice of the presence of people (and of God) is the answer to all our problems.

We tend to treat problems as if they were mental conundrums, puzzles to be worked through by independent reasoning. But behind every question lies a better question, and ultimately every question takes the shape of a human face. Every problem, in other words, has a relational root. The only real problem in the world is alienation, and the only cure is love. Questions are answered and problems solved only as we come into right relationship with people.

I had an agnostic uncle who used to say, "There are no answers, there are only questions." To this my answer is, "There are no questions, there are only people."

How else to say this? The poet William Carlos Williams valued concrete realism so highly that he sought to free his writing from all

42

abstractions. He expressed this goal in his famous poetic dictum, "No ideas but in things." I suggest taking this one step further to say, "No answers but in people."

Picture your life as a dark forest in which you are lost. How are you to find your way? You may wish the forest was not there, but it is. You may wish for some magical intervention, but this is not likely to happen. No, you yourself must find the way. Beginning where you are, you must discern some light in the shadows, decide on a path, and follow it.

Peering closely at the trees around you, gradually you realize that these are not trees at all, but people! Each one of these trees has a face, and each face has a light in it.

Isn't this true? Aren't we lost in a forest of people? Perhaps the people who could help us most are the ones we despise or ignore because we do not see the light in them. If we were drowning, and these same people were all around us in the water, wouldn't we reach out to them? We wouldn't worry then about how little we have in common!

The forest in which we are lost is a forest of relationships—or more precisely, nonrelationships. We may think our problems have to do with finances, work, health, or something else. But our real problem is people. Problems do not have abstract, philosophical solutions. The answer to each problem is a person.

Most of us try to solve our problems without recourse to relationships. We search and search for a diet that will work, a job that will satisfy, a method for overcoming insomnia, a secure and happy place to live. Of course, we'll admit we have people problems, too, but we'll never quite do what it takes to resolve these. By trying to locate the answers in ourselves rather than in healed relationships, we stop short of achieving real peace.

Since our fundamental need is for love, every personal problem is interpersonal. Those problems that do not seem to be connected to people are actually awaiting a relational resolution. Our desperate campaign to resolve these issues on our own is doomed to failure. Our questions will never be answered if we insist on asking them in isolation.

Problems are not what we think. They are problems because we are looking at them in the wrong way. Typically we struggle with surface symptoms rather than delving for the root. When a logjam blocks a river, thousands of logs can be removed from the middle of the jam without effecting any change. But zero in on one key log at the front, and the whole shebang gives way.

This is how it is with the troublesome people in our lives. A single damaged relationship, once restored to health, will solve a wide-ranging nexus of apparently unrelated personal problems. The problems are nothing; it's the people behind them who count.

Who are the key logs in your life? Father, mother, and siblings are a good place to start. If only you understood the blessing that awaits you when brothers and sisters become friends instead of rivals! Or when your parents become real people to you rather than estranged ghosts!

Try traveling halfway around the world to get in touch with that old grandmother of yours, and see what chronic disorders will vanish from your life like mist. Then move on to the boss who wronged you, the friend who deserted you, the cousin who abused you, and so on. Think of the agony you feel when you have a fight with someone you are close to right now—your spouse, a child, a good friend. Do you not realize that the same agony clings unresolved to every broken relationship from the past? The pain still rankles. You cope with it and pretend it is not there, but it *is* there and will continue to fester until you deal with it.

A sign in a remedial education center reads: "Few people understand the courage it takes for a child to return to a place where he failed yesterday and the day before and will probably fail again." But to avoid resolving the failed relationships of the past is to keep on failing in the present. The healing of past relationships needn't always be done in person, nor does it mean becoming buddy-buddy with our abusers and betrayers. But as the faces of our life float before us, we'll know what to do to make our peace with each one. We forgive people not because they deserve our forgiveness, but because we want to be free.

Make friends with your past. Let the story of your life be a biography of joy and victory, not a trail of broken dreams. Forgive the dream-crusher, and no one will ever crush your dreams again.

CHAPTER 10

Needing People

Whether we love people or not, we still need them. Indeed it often happens that the one we need most is the one we love least.

Once while attending a conference I received some news that left me shaken. Knowing my need to reach out to others, I deliberately sought out two friends whom I knew I could count on for help. Each listened to my trouble and compassionately counseled and prayed for me. But for some reason this did not help. A few hours later I was feeling more distraught than ever. At that point I happened to be sitting beside a man to whom I'd taken a dislike. I'd judged him as a self-centered talker and a bore. Yet now, in a moment of panic, I turned to him and spilled out my woes. He then took my hands, looked into my eyes, and spoke words that lifted me out of despair. To him God had given the key to my trouble.

Again and again I receive unexpected help from the unlikeliest of sources. People I've judged often hold the greatest gifts for me. What an incentive this becomes to surrender all judgments, especially those that would place us above the help of people we perceive as being weaker. Counselors, social workers, teachers, or missionaries become most effective when they open up to receive help from those they seek to help.

People who do not need people, do not love. We do not really begin to love until the day comes when we deeply need someone, when some particular person becomes, in a sense, our salvation, rescuing us out of some desperate need. To feel lost and then to feel the touch of another human being reaching toward us across the gulf, not out of strength but often out of mutual frailty—this is an unforgettable experience. A bond is forged that cannot be forged in any other way. Until this happens to us in church, what reason would we have to feel we belong? Until it happens in our neighborhood, what reason is there to join the human race?

In our independent society it is risky to acknowledge our dependence on others. When we drop hints about our need for help, and then feel misunderstood or rejected, often we react by distancing ourselves and rejecting in turn. The apostle Paul, however, shows us a different way. Paul openly acknowledged his need of others, but when his feelings were not reciprocated he did not react by writing people off. Rather he continued to yearn for them, soliciting their love not out of his own suffering but out of genuine affection. "We have spoken freely to you, Corinthians, and opened wide our hearts to you. We are not withholding our affection from you, but you are withholding yours from us" (2 Corinthians 6:11-12).

In Paul we see a man who experienced tremendous pain in his relationships without giving way to bitterness. We see a man so keenly aware of the blessing that could come to him through the whole body of Christ that whenever anyone broke the circle of love he felt it as a personal loss. In short, Paul not only needed people, he wanted them. More than striving toward his own spiritual perfection, he was striving toward a community of love, toward church.

CHAPTER 11

Wanting People

G od did not create people out of need but because He wanted
to, just for the love of it. Strictly speaking, I do not know that
I am needed in this world. But as God's child I do know that I
am wanted. It seems to me that the world could carry on quite well
without me. Would it make any difference if there were one less star
in the heavens? No, that extra star is not there because it is needed,
but because it is wanted. It is there because Someone wanted it.

Knowing I am wanted, both by God and by other people, is
more mysterious and freeing than being needed. Similarly, it is better
for me to want God and to want people than to relate out of need.
Want is a purer and a higher idea than need, or than should, ought,
or must.

Christian growth involves eliminating all the shoulds and the
oughts from life and replacing them with wants. Imagine building
your life around only those things you want to do, only the things
you love! It sounds too good to be true, but in fact this is the essence
of the gospel. Having "died to the law" with all its demands (Galatians 2:19), "delight yourself in the LORD and he will give you the

desires of your heart" (Psalm 37:4). Those deep desires are there because the Lord put them there and He wants you to have them. They are His desires first; He created them. As the beautiful pattern of grace comes full circle in your life, it turns out that what God wants for you is exactly what you want most deeply for yourself.

What could be better than living purely for the love of it? Wouldn't you like to eliminate all need and do exactly as you please? Granted, in the Garden of Eden we got off on the wrong foot. Satan convinced us to do something we did not really want to do, and so there entered into our nature a twisted idea of want. This false desire, called sin, obscures and encrusts the true desires of our heart.

The way to follow Christ is to peel off the crust and to pursue what we truly want. What is this deepest of all desires? It is nothing short of love.

To love is to want others as we ourselves long to be wanted. Are there people in your life you do not want? Either learn to want them, or else forget them. Wouldn't it be better to send them away than to pretend you want them when you do not? Why sit on the fence?

Most of us sit on the fence in regard to people, neither whole-heartedly wanting them nor sullenly retreating to a hermitage. If we get along with others, it tends to be more out of need than want. This is one problem Jesus came into the world to redress. He let us crucify Him to show us how much we push everyone away, even the Son of God. As the dust settled on Calvary, some of us realized what we were missing. We realized how much we wanted love and how much He wanted us. And so we invited Him to come back and live in our hearts.

When He did, something wonderful happened: We began to

wake up to how badly we'd been treating people and how much we missed each other. We began to want one another with a deep, pure love. And so the church was born.

Peter writes of this mystery, "Now that you have purified yourselves by obeying the truth so that you have sincere love for your brothers, love one another deeply, from the heart" (1 Peter 1:22). Peter's exhortation is to obey not rituals or regulations, but "the truth," which is the good news of God's love and forgiveness through Jesus Christ. You can know when you are obeying the truth, says Peter, because the result will be sincere love.

Peter's words have a sobering corollary: If you do not have sincere love for people, and if that love is not daily growing deeper and fresher, then it can only be because you are not obeying the truth. Your life may be morally sound and you may be a good churchgoer with all the right theology, but if the result is not a clean, free conscience overflowing with pure love, then something is wrong.

CHAPTER 12

Mother Teresa

Mother Teresa gave her life to wanting the unwanted. In caring for the poorest of the poor, she was remembering something that had been forgotten: people. She went to gutters and garbage heaps, to places where humanity itself had been thrown away and left to rot, and there she set to work patiently and tenderly restoring to people the dignity of being human.

If Mother Teresa could do this for people whose toes and fingers were nibbled by rats and whose living flesh crawled with maggots, then can you and I not do the same for the healthy and attractive people who are our friends and neighbors? Can we not make it our goal to give some dignity to everyone we meet, to encounter others in a way that leaves them actually feeling more human, more loved?

We will never be motivated to do this until we see the image of God in people. All of Mother Teresa's days began with prayer, and after meeting God in prayer she went out into the streets of Calcutta to meet Him there in the form of people. The people she cared for were Christ to her. She took with absolute literalness Jesus' words,

"Whatever you did for one of the least of these brothers of mine, you did for me" (Matthew 25:40).

During the 1980s the paintings of Michelangelo in the Sistine Chapel underwent restoration. Centuries of accumulated soot and grime were removed, revealing astonishingly vivid colors underneath. A panoply of figures that the world had not even seen as being smudged and dark were suddenly filled with light.

What was done in Rome for painted images, Mother Teresa did in Calcutta for living souls. Her primary goal was not to better the lot of the poor, not to alleviate the suffering of the sick, not even to save lives. Rather, her goal was to recover the image of God in people. For this work her primary tool was not food, clothing, money, or orphanages, but God's love. "It's not how much you do that counts," she said, "but how much love is in what you do."

She went to the very poorest people because these were the ones to whom God had called her. Who are your people? Who is calling out for your love? Perhaps it is the comfortable middle-class people in your own neighborhood or family. In Mother Teresa's eyes it was not a better thing to serve the poor than the rich. She was merely following her vocation. "A vocation cannot be forced," she said. "It comes from above."

In the eyes of the rich, Mother Teresa saw the same loneliness, the same poverty, the same desperation as in the poor. "The world is suffering much," she said, "because of this terrible disease—not of leprosy, not of tuberculosis, not even of hunger—but of that feeling of wanting to be wanted, to be loved, to be somebody to somebody." Not only in the streets of Calcutta, but in North America, too,

Mother Teresa saw faces filled with pain, disease, abandonment, abject poverty. Jesus said the same: "You do not realize that you are wretched, pitiful, poor, blind and naked" (Revelation 3:17).

Since the rich have the same basic needs as the poor, they require the same treatment. They too need to be touched, to be smiled at, to be taken into someone's heart, to feel the purity of love. The self-reliant and the strong, perhaps even more than the weak, need to be somebody to somebody. Who is prepared to work at restoring true dignity to these gray and careworn faces, these puffy, overweight bodies, these frantic and frightened lives?

The light of God is a lamp whose fuel is human flesh. The flame is within; it matters not how the flesh looks on the outside. Mother Teresa looked past the present, surface appearance of people to see into their past and future. She saw their beautiful, innocent past in the Garden of Eden, and she saw their glorious potential as the children of God in heaven. Seeing the light of God's image deep down in human beings, she devoted herself to lovingly cleaning away the smudge and grime of poverty and neglect so that this true light could shine. Sure enough, as she gently touched the destitute and the dying and cleaned their wounds, an actual light seemed to glow in them. Many who have visited her houses of charity have spoken of the otherworldly radiance in these dim, ugly, unlikely places.

Can the presence of God be seen and felt? Yes, there is a light and a warmth where true love is present. It is the light of Christ, as spoken of in the first chapter of John: "In him was life, and that life was the light of men. The light shines in the darkness, but the darkness has not understood it" (vv. 4-5).

God can be seen. But do we have eyes to see?

Sometimes in the woods I'll see a wildflower, perhaps one that has just blossomed that morning, and I'll think: *No one has ever laid eyes on this flower before.* A strange purity dwells where human eyes have never touched. In the same way, are there not millions of people in the world whom no one has ever seen, whom no eyes have ever touched with deep, pure love? Perhaps we do not need to do anything else for these people except to see them, to notice them. If only we would open our eyes, our hearts too would open like flowers and the perfume of good deeds would flow.

CHAPTER 13

Death

I have a rare and precious possession: a tape recording of a conversation between my mother, my grandmother, my grand-
father, and a favorite uncle. All these people are dead now. How
amazing that I can still hear their voices! This is not the only recording I have of these voices, but it is one of few, and it's the only one
that brings all these people together.

I first listened to this tape shortly after my mother's death. My
heart was soft and open, and when I heard my mother's voice it was
like hearing the first bird call on a spring morning of exquisite, otherworldly beauty. I was astounded at the purity of that voice, at its rich
array of tonal colors, and at the wealth of character revealed in that
sound. My mother's voice brought back to me her whole person, not
just as I had known her, but as she really was. Here she was in her
perfected state, as if all the ideals she had held so dear in her heart of
hearts, all her most treasured beliefs and dreams, had not been in the
least thwarted, but had been fully realized. Here was the whole, true
person I had never seen, the perfect woman she herself had longed
to be.

Suddenly I realized what a voice is: the music of the soul. Words can conceal, but the voice, like fingerprints, identifies the true person. Why had I never noticed this before? In all the years of listening to my mother's voice, never had I heard her this way. Never before had I fallen in love with the mere sound of her voice.

All the voices on the tape were like this. Though the others were not quite so dear to me as my mother's, each one leapt to life as if the person were being resurrected before my eyes. How awesome and precious these people were! Listening to them now was like sitting among kings and queens. I could vividly picture the room in which the recording was made, the living room of my uncle's apartment in Toronto, the same room in which I had often visited with these relatives over the years. Yet never before had I experienced them as I did now. Never before had I so deeply understood and cherished them, nor felt so intimately connected, nor been so grateful for their lives. How blind I had been! How deaf! Though all were now dead, suddenly I felt that they were alive while I was the one who dwelt in the shadows.

How odd that now, simply through the sound of voices on a tape recorder, I could experience the fullness of these lives as I never had in countless face-to-face meetings. What had changed? What was the difference, I wondered, between then and now?

The difference was that now my heart was soft and open. I was now in a place where I could love richly and purely.

Death, it is said, wonderfully concentrates the mind. Sadly and paradoxically, we never practice a person's presence so intently as when that one is gone. It's almost as if, by summoning all our powers of memory and concentration, we could bring that person back and keep him or her with us. If only we could love in life as we do in death!

As it is, we are pinched and stingy with our love. We treat love like money, as if there's never enough to go around, and so we draw our heartstrings tighter than our purse strings. How can we grasp that we are dealing with an inexhaustible currency? Hate will exhaust itself, but love never will. Hate and indifference will run down into death, but love is eternal life.

The sign that we are practicing the presence of people is that they begin to become infinitely precious to us. The sound of a voice, the color and glow of skin, that look in the eyes that is theirs and theirs alone, the smallest detail of expression and mannerism—everything about those we love is more eloquent and fascinating than the greatest works of art. Gazing with love upon the visible, we begin to see invisible qualities, too, and gradually the very soul opens to us like a flower.

This priceless flower remains hidden to everything but pure love. Why not open the eyes of love right now? Why not open our hearts wide today, in the living presence of our loved ones, rather than procrastinating until they're gone? Why wait for death's cruel crowbar to pry the lid off our true feelings? Why not let people be infinitely precious to us right now? Now is the time to eulogize. Now is the time to deck with flowers. Today is the day to bear to its rest the whole weight of our love's flesh upon our shoulders.

CHAPTER 14

Practicing the Presence of Brother Lawrence

A wise teacher at Regent College, James Houston, once recommended to me that rather than reading many spiritual books, I should choose one and simply follow that one, reading it over and over and working it unto my life. For years I avoided this good advice until finally it caught up with me in the form of Brother Lawrence. His simple ideas began to exercise a pull on me such as no other writing ever had, and so I decided to stick with this one book until I had done my best to absorb and to practice everything in it.

Why are we so fickle with books? Only because we do not want to practice what they preach. We think that all we need to do is read a book and its ideas will sink into us by osmosis. Even writers may assume they know something simply because they have written a book about it! But true wisdom is not a matter of thinking lofty thoughts, but of living them out. Brother Lawrence observed, "One must carefully differentiate between the actions of the understanding and those of the will: for the former are of little value and the latter, all."[4]

We all have books on our shelves that we have never read. Some people actually persuade themselves that they have read these books merely because they possess them. Sadly, many treat their friends the same way. The way we relate to books says a great deal about the way we relate to people. If we are serious about practicing the wisdom found in books, then we will learn to be faithful to a good book as to a good friend. We will keep such a book in our lives rather than on the shelf. The gate of learning is not the mind but the will. When a book begins to speak to us, we know it is time to act.

Obviously this is the point of reading the Bible. Again and again Jesus exhorts us not only to listen to His words but to put them into practice, for by doing so we enter into a relationship with the author. Has it ever occurred to us that the same is true of other good books? It matters not how much or how little we read. What counts is whether we enter into a living relationship with the author. For we do not learn *from* others so much as *through* them; we grow not on our own but in relationship. All true wisdom is relational. If an idea is really true, it will draw us closer to others.

Because the act of reading is done alone, it can seem deceptively solitary. But if reading is not a soft, intimate, and relational activity, it will stagnate and die. I'm reminded again of some advice of James Houston: "Don't just read books—spend time with the authors." In the case of Brother Lawrence, it came as a thunderous revelation to me that I did not have to settle for simply reading his book, but I could actually take him to my heart as a friend.

The heart is the mysterious meeting ground where we come to know others through realizing our oneness with them. Are not all Christians, whether on earth or in heaven, "one in Christ Jesus" (Galatians 3:28)? Years ago I asked Jesus into my heart. Then at church I began to experience being "one in heart" (Acts 4:32) with other believers. Later I gave my heart to a woman in holy matrimony. Now, through Brother Lawrence who went to his reward in 1691, I'm learning something of participating in the communion of saints in glory.

Thus began my mystical friendship with Brother Lawrence—a friendship that I trust will be everlasting. After this, reading his book became a different experience, for I found that his ideas took on an actual life. Now I was not just admiring and agreeing with what I read, but finding the power to put it into practice.

During the writing of this book, I've felt at times as if Brother Lawrence himself were at my side, smiling encouragement. I even feel that if he were alive today and could write a second book, he might call it *Practicing the Presence of People*. And so my own book was born.

SELF

*Although you think it is yourself you are doubting,
you are really doubting the Lord.*

HANNAH WHITALL SMITH

*T*he photographer stands in the park with his subject. It is a beautiful day, a perfect day for a picture. But the subject is nervous, ill at ease. The photographer knows that his first and most difficult job is to get his subject to relax, to be herself. Until this happens, all his film will be wasted.

The photographer takes a few pictures anyway, just to fool the subject into thinking that the session is proceeding well. *This may not be so bad,* she begins to think.

"Turn this way," the photographer says. "Now that way.... Now lift your right arm a little.... Now let's try a different angle, against those trees.... Good.... Very good."

It's not really very good. The photographer knows he hasn't yet got what he wants. Far from it. There's one shot he's looking for. Just one.

What is it? What does he want? He wants a revelation of character. He's looking for the subject to be entirely herself, to reveal in one unguarded moment who she is. The photographer knows that this can only happen in an unguarded moment, because the subject, like most people, is fiercely protective of her true identity. She herself does not know who she is, let alone give out this information to others. It is a secret.

The art of the photographer is to bring this deep, dark secret out into the open and expose it with a flash of light. To accomplish this is more difficult than to photograph the rarest of wild animals in the jungle. At least a lion, if you can get a look at one, looks like a lion. But people so seldom look like themselves. To look ourselves, we have to feel ourselves, to feel comfortable and at home in our own flesh. To be fully and unself-consciously alive—what wouldn't we give to feel this for one moment, let alone to live this way? Yet for most of us this is the rare exception, not the rule.

The photographer is looking for the exception. The world lives by rules, but the artist looks for exceptions. We all know the exceptional to see it, because it stands out. It feels different, looks different. It *is* different. It has a quality all its own. It is like nothing else. Call it truth, call it freedom, call it reality. But when it happens, you know it.

All of us at times experience our true selves. Within each of us lies the capacity to be free and alive, but we don't like to let on. Why not? Because as long as the cat's in the bag, we can pretend it's not there. But let the cat out for one minute, and we might never get it stuffed back in. We might be changed, utterly and forever! How frightening! A little taste of reality is fine. But the thought of living our whole life in the glaring light of day... No, this is too much.

People are afraid of themselves, afraid of living freely. Oh, we like the feeling of freedom whenever it comes to us serendipitously. But we don't want to take responsibility for it. We don't want to have to *live* that way. We are frightened of the implications, frightened of the revolution we might be caught up in. Why, anything might happen! We might have to dance in the streets, or go skinny-dipping, or say no to our bosses or our wives, or take a whole day to sit in a meadow gazing at wildflowers. We might have to spend some money, or stop spending. We might have to put a rose in our teeth and go around hugging strangers.

What would it be for you? What would you have to do, right now, to express the real you? How could you snatch some freedom from this day and run with it? Be honest. When you're living authentically, you know it. You can feel it in your bones. You're alive in every cell. You feel your deep, true self breach the waves and flash joyous and impossible in the sunlight.

"The wind blows wherever it pleases," said Jesus to a stuffed shirt named Nicodemus. "You hear its sound, but you cannot tell where it comes from or where it is going. So it is with everyone born of the Spirit" (John 3:8). Reading these words, I think of Jesus Himself, of what it might be like to be in the same room with Him. I see someone astoundingly free, wholly unpredictable, now here and now there, saying and doing whatever He jolly well likes.

How about you? Knowing how different you are from every other person in the world can leave you feeling isolated and paralyzed. Why not do a little blowing like the wind? Maybe you need to put on some dance music and feel in your body what it could be like to live without walls. Or maybe you need to blow verbally, asking a friend to listen for an hour or so while you vent all that is inside you without restraint.

Where is the environment that is safe enough for you to experiment with total freedom? All you need is one place in your life where you can blow like the wind. Take the lid off an empty jar and give the dead air inside a sniff of the fresh, the big, the real, the free air outside. One small taste of how good life can be will ruin forever a trapped and boring existence.

Once you have "tasted that the Lord is good," Peter advises: "Like newborn babies, crave pure spiritual milk, so that by it you may grow up in your salvation" (1 Peter 2:2-3). Many talk of being "born again," but how many are growing up? The new birth is just the first little taste, the barest beginning of life. Once we get a feel for who we really are, there's no stopping. As my first pastor, Harry Robinson, once commented to me, "God's purposes for us are so unlimited that there's no time for coasting."

The problem is not just that we do not know ourselves, but that we do not love ourselves. That's why we keep ourselves locked up in a little black box and have to be surprised into letting the secret out. If only we'd take some time to listen to the Holy Spirit, we'd begin to hear Him say, "Turn this way.... Now look that way.... Now lift your chin...." He works with us kindly, patiently, pose after pose, until the magical moment comes, the glimmer of revelation. As the shutter clicks, we may not even realize what has happened; it may take some time for the picture to develop. But as we enter the darkroom with the mysterious photographer and peer over His shoulder at the emerging image, suddenly, with a shiver of recognition, we'll cry out, *"Yes! That's me!"*

CHAPTER 15

Loving Yourself

*P*erhaps you are thinking: We spend so much time focusing on ourselves. Isn't the goal of practicing the presence of people to release us from this neurotic squirrel cage? Isn't it true that the way to know myself is not to look in the mirror, but to love someone? Why then a chapter on loving myself?

Because your self, redeemed in Christ, is what you love with. The self is the tool with which you practice the presence of others. If you are not good at being yourself, you won't be good at letting others be who they are.

Consider Jesus' command, "Love your neighbor as yourself." The commands of Jesus are not like the commands of a general to his army; they are not like human commands at all. Rather, Jesus' commands are plain statements of truth. A light goes on and you see the truth of the thing, and then you begin to do it as naturally as breathing. If you do not first see the truth, you will never obey the command. You cannot.

Jesus' second great commandment implies that we will love others only to the extent that we love ourselves. The command might be better understood by putting the words "You will" in front of it: "*You will* love your neighbor as yourself." That is, the feelings you have toward yourself will inevitably be projected upon others. If you do not love yourself, you will not love your neighbor. If you are not real to yourself, no one else will be real to you either. This is not a command as we normally think of commands; rather, it is the way things are. It is a natural law. You will not and cannot treat others any better than you treat yourself. Why would you?

It is a monstrous lie to think that I can be anything to others that I am not to myself. If I am not gentle with myself, I will not be gentle with others. If I am not generous to myself, neither will I give to anyone else. If I am plagued with guilt, be it ever so subtly, then I will be harsh and judgmental with others. Moreover everyone around me will be aware of my critical nature, while I myself will be the last to know.

To the servant who put his talent to good use and earned ten more, the Master said, "Because you have been trustworthy in a very small matter, take charge of ten cities" (Luke 19:17). The first small matter we must look to is ourselves. Yet how many people ever learn to take good care of this one poor, small thing? We want to help and heal the whole world, but we will not start with ourselves.

How can we know if we love ourselves? What is the sign? It's simple: We'll have lives that are characterized by being warm and full inside, happy and thankful.

What? Who ever heard of such foolishness! Warm and happy—in a world like this? Nonsense!

Yes, the extremity of our reaction gives us away. The degree of our shock will register how thoroughly we have bought the lie that it is not okay to look after ourselves. Far from feeling warm and content and full of gratitude, we spend our days being stressed, insecure, angry, sullen, or numb with genteel denial. And in this condition we continue to tell ourselves that we can work, love, be productive, smile, help others, make a difference. But it's all a sickening lie.

The way to make a difference in this world is to become what everyone else is not: happy and full of life. It's not enough just to point the way; we must become the way, as Jesus was. He made it possible for us to have "the full measure of [His] joy" within us (John 17:13). Why aren't we filling up our tanks? Is it because we won't admit we are empty? Are we so proud and neurotic that we cannot even believe that joy—real joy, irrepressibly bubbling over—is deservedly ours? Shutting ourselves off from this fullness, we have nothing to share with anyone else. Moreover, if we're not filling up with joy ourselves, it's guaranteed we're taking it from others. We are robbing each other blind.

CHAPTER 16

Beautiful You

Love for self is not selfishness, because the way I see myself is like a pair of glasses through which I look at the world. If my image of myself is poor, then my vision will be warped so that I cannot see beauty in others. But if I see myself as God sees me, with lovingkindness, then I will see everyone else through these same glasses. "The eye is the lamp of the body," taught Jesus. "If your eyes are good, your whole body will be full of light. But if your eyes are bad, your whole body will be full of darkness" (Matthew 6:22-23).

Love is not a tool, like a lamp or a pair of glasses, but love requires tools to be implemented. A smile, a hug, a timely letter or phone call—these are some of the tools that help love to become incarnate. But the ultimate tool for implementing love is my own image of myself. My body may be fat, but if I see myself as beautiful, my obesity will never isolate me from others. Even losing weight will not make me happy unless I first see myself as beautiful already, just the way I am. Good dieting begins with self-respect. Then the diet is not a form of self-punishment but of reward.

It is never good to punish ourselves. Yet we do it all the time and feel justified about it. *I know I do not really love others as I should,* we think with pious self-judgment. How sadly ironic this is—for the reason we do not love others as we should is that we are so hard on ourselves for not doing it! If we loved ourselves, we would not morbidly dwell upon our shortcomings, but simply confess them and be free. Like Brother Lawrence we would have compassion for our failings: "Whenever he stumbled he quickly acknowledged his fault and said to God, 'I shall never do otherwise if You leave me to myself; it is up to You to keep me from falling and to correct what is wrong.' With this he put the pain of this fault from his mind."[1]

When we get bogged down in self-punishment, we are setting ourselves up as judge. But there is only one Judge, and that is God. "I do not even judge myself," wrote Paul. "It is the Lord who judges me" (1 Corinthians 4:3-4). The Lord's judgment of me is that, through the blood of Jesus Christ, all my sin is forgiven. If I sit in God's place and continue to judge myself, I nullify the gospel. Moreover, pouring contempt on myself ensures that I will treat others just as harshly.

When it comes to guilt and condemnation, we should all regard ourselves as alcoholics. One little sip of the stuff goes straight to our heads and we lose all perspective. In our younger days, perhaps, the effects of our addiction didn't seem so ravaging. We thought we could handle it. But now the dragon has caught up with us. We have a progressive, fatal illness for which there is only one cure: Don't take that first drink! Stay away from condemnation! One sip ruins our freedom.

Self-condemnation never works; it only digs the hole deeper. Though we may feel pious, we're indulging in a weak-willed excuse for not living life to the full. Sitting sullenly atop our own dung pile, we cut ourselves off from God's love. Meanwhile our Father is inviting us to get up and walk into the light, to come and live in a place that is beyond all shame. This place is our righteousness in Christ. In Christ we are redeemed, washed, born again, made pure and holy. This is who we are. Through faith we gain a new identity. When we spend energy accusing ourselves of being unrighteous, we are identifying with our old, false selves, not with the newborn child of God.

"Let us return into ourselves," urges Brother Lawrence, and in the same sentence he tells how: "Let us make way for grace, let us break this dike that dams it."[2] To do this we must overcome the one great obstacle in our path—our sin. Subconsciously we ask ourselves: How can I ever be comfortable with myself, knowing how bad I am? How can I live a beautiful life filled with love, when I know that I am damaged and imperfect? How can I even see beauty when my glasses are all smudged and broken? Why even try?

But here is the secret: Your smudged and damaged self is not the tool with which you take hold of love; the tool, rather, is the way you see that broken person. The tool, in other words, is self-forgiveness, which in turn makes way for self-love. If you can forgive and love yourself, "the greatest of sinners," you can love anyone. As author Paul Hiebert once said to me of his ninety-year-old wife, "I don't love her because she's beautiful. She's beautiful because I love her."

So you have a big ugly nose? Love that nose, and when you do you will love every nose in the world. Jimmy Durante built an entire career out of loving his nose. His worst feature became his own favorite part of himself, his very signature. In fact if you go to Mann's

Chinese Theater in Hollywood, you can see the profile of Durante's big schnoz pressed into cement. If Jimmy had hated his nose and hidden behind shame, he would have spent his life secretly despising other people for their good-looking noses, their good-looking faces, their successful lives. Instead Jimmy's embarrassing weakness became his tool for reaching out and touching others and creating laughter.

CHAPTER 17

Loving What
You Love

D on't sit around wondering whether you love yourself. Just do it! Take yourself dancing. Smell the flowers. Do something fun right now. If you felt attracted to a woman and asked her for a date, she might say no. You could be rejected. But with yourself there's no need for this problem. Why go on rejecting yourself? Ask yourself out on a date tonight and say yes! Jump at the chance! Buy yourself a small present. Pay yourself some compliments. Treat yourself as you would a gorgeous woman or a handsome gentleman. Be courteous, kind, generous, and intrigued. Feel honored to be in your presence.

Come now, what would it take for you and yourself to have a wonderful time together, starting now? What would you love to do that you're denying yourself? Don't get stuck on all those seemingly impossible dreams. For now, explore real possibilities. Decide on something that would work and do it. It doesn't have to be big or take a lot of time. If you've been heavily into self-denial, you'll want to start small.

For example, don't suddenly decide to quit your job, even if it's killing you. That can come later. Instead you might choose to take one day a week, or even one afternoon, to do something special to pamper yourself. Pick something simple and doable that you *know* will be fun. Something where you won't have to keep wondering, *Am I really enjoying myself, or not?* Listen: You *do know* how to enjoy yourself. The only problem is that you don't do it. You waste your time on things that ought to feel good but don't. Stop kidding yourself. Get real. Love what you love.

Maybe for you it's walking on the beach, or building a sandcastle, or flying a Japanese fighter kite. Maybe it's finger painting or mucking with clay. Maybe it's just sitting still with a cup of coffee and gazing out the window. What would it take to get in touch with the soft, precious core of the real you?

A date with yourself doesn't have to be elaborate or expensive. When two people fall in love, it's not usually in the midst of heli-skiing. No, they're sitting at a little table somewhere, oblivious of their surroundings but absorbed in one another. When was the last time you looked with fascination into your own eyes or listened attentively to your deeper thoughts? Why not put your arms around your knees right now and hug and kiss them? Stop shutting yourself out. Give yourself some love.

Love yourself, and then you will have love for others. If I want to be charitable with money, I must have money to give away. If I want to be charitable with love, joy, and peace, my own bank account must have a surplus. I must be a calm, happy, cherished person.

"But how can I be happy?" you ask. This is the wrong question. Instead you should ask, "How can I touch happiness with my little finger?" You do not have joy because you see it as a large and impossible achievement rather than something small, obvious, and practical. "Find out what pleases the Lord," says the Bible (Ephesians 5:10). The same goes for yourself. Find out what you love, richly and deeply in your own unique way, and spend time doing it. Try doing it for just one hour, and feel what it's like to feel good, to be alive and curious, relaxed and at peace.

Once your inner photographer has snapped a few pictures of the real you, you can begin to run the stills together into a movie. Having enjoyed yourself for an hour, you can do it for two, or for an evening. Then make a day of it. Spend time with yourself; give yourself a chance to fall in love. This is practicing your presence, walking in the light of your true self. Slowly, little by little, you will see that it is more fun to be good to yourself than not to. It works better. Do it more and more, and before long you will find that you have built up enough bold-hearted exuberance to quit that job that's been killing you and to start living your dreams.

But start small. Learn to touch joy with your little finger. Most people remain paralyzed by huge dreams they cannot achieve, yet they will not take the small, practical baby steps that would lead in that direction. "Who despises the day of small things?" (Zechariah 4:10). Love is a big thing, but it is made up of small, daily actions, simple words, shared intimacies. Love is a necklace forged of intimate moments. When the chain is broken and the beads scatter, there is nothing to do but get down on your knees and string it again, one precious bead at a time.

CHAPTER 18

Slowing Down

Loving yourself has a lot to do with slowing down. Have you ever noticed that no matter how full your days are, you always try to add one thing more? This gives all your days the feel of burdens to which one straw too many has been added. The Peter Principle tends to be true: Everyone rises to the level of their incompetence. Why not take yourself down a peg or two, and spend your energy doing what you can instead of what you can't? Rather than adding one thing more every day, why not try adding one thing less?

One of my favorite authors, Annie Dillard, advises young writers to cut out the unnecessary words from every sentence. "A sentence is a machine," she writes; "it has a job to do. An extra word in a sentence is like a sock in a machine."[3] The same is true of extraneous deeds in a day. Try editing your days; craft them to sing concisely like memorable lines of poetry. The elimination of that one stocking stuffer may be all it takes.

Rushing is anxiety in motion. For years I tried to break the habit of rushing but couldn't. Then one day I sprained my ankle and was forced to slow down. As with any setback, I couldn't understand why

God had allowed this to happen. To me it was just a huge inconvenience, even an insult. But there was no use complaining. Instead I had to adjust my lifestyle and learn to be gentle with myself. Literally having to think about every step I took, my actions became slow and deliberate.

After eight weeks of this, I realized I had given up on rushing. The forced change in my external habits had resulted in a profound internal change. This happened so gradually that I hardly noticed it until one day when I was shaving. Always I'd resented the need to shave and hurried distractedly through it. But now as I scraped the razor over my skin, I found myself studying my face in the mirror, peering into my own eyes, feeling the creamy texture of my flesh, wondering at my own living clay. In these few moments the miracle of life jumped out at me. It was like taking down a pottery vase from the cupboard and having it suddenly grow warm, move, smile, and speak. I could even see the marks, still fresh, of the Potter's own fingers embedded in my eye sockets, along the creases of my nose, and in the intricate coils of my ears.

Another day I was standing in the shower feeling the warm water run all over me like melting flesh. Suddenly, peering down at my naked feet, I realized how beautiful they were! Their veins stood out like soft blue wires, and wiggling my toes I could see the fine network of bones rippling below the surface like rigging in a breeze. How was it my entire body managed to balance itself on these two small, delicate pads? Lifting one foot (the unsprained one), I stood like a wand of kelp waving in the current, like a Japanese crane, head bowed as in prayer, lost in wonder at this simple balancing act on a once-injured member. Watching the water run down my leg and pool around that one astoundingly beautiful foot, I came close to tears. This was a foot that Jesus was washing!

In short, in the midst of the most ordinary activities, I found myself indulging in the practice of my own presence. Through the injury to my ankle, a new gentleness had crept into all my bones like oil. Something deep inside me had relaxed. While initially I had viewed my sprain as an insult, now I saw that the real insult was all the frantic rushing I had done in my lifetime, the enormous pressure I had kept myself under. Living this way was like always trying to squeeze myself into a too-small pair of pants.

Tolstoy wrote a famous story entitled "How Much Land Does a Man Need?" In it a man strikes a deal whereby he may claim as much land as he is able to cover on foot between sunrise and sunset of one day. The only stipulation is that he must return to the same spot by sundown. Of course, the man bites off more than he can chew and in the process completely exhausts himself. Though in the end he manages to crawl back to the starting point, he dies upon arrival. How much land did he need then? Six feet.

How many hours do you need in a day? Would twenty-five be enough? How about thirty or forty? With enough extra hours, could you afford to stop rushing around? Or would you still crawl into bed each night exhausted with greed?

CHAPTER 19

Contemplation

Walt Whitman's poem "Song of Myself" begins with the line, "I lean and loaf at my ease observing a spear of summer grass." This is not a bad way to begin to practice your own presence. If you feel that God doesn't speak to you, ask yourself: When do I ever lean and loaf at my ease to enjoy something beautiful for its own sake? Do I even know how to be at ease for one minute?

Contemplation is the ABC of prayer. Just as all language is formed from the alphabet, so all prayer—whether worship, confession, thanksgiving, or intercession—flows out of the stillness of contemplation. Far from being a "high" form of prayer, contemplation is the simplest form. Contemplation is the prayer that all of us do naturally, without thinking. If we could notice what we are doing when we are not thinking and do more of it, our prayer lives would move ahead wondrously!

The trouble is that most of us insist on doing things we do not do well or spontaneously. We think that if something is too easy or natural, it won't count. In this way we devalue our true gifts. Don't let the term *spiritual gifts* mislead you into expecting something dramatic or unnatural. The gifts of God are supernatural in origin, but in their operation they are as beautifully natural as a summer's day. Every believer has a natural gift for prayer, but we will not know about it until we relax enough to do what comes naturally.

A prayer life is like a voice or a face. We may long for the face of a model, but this will not change the way we actually look. God wants us to turn to Him the face He sees, the one that is ours and ours alone. Similarly He does not want us to speak to Him in a high squeaky voice or to affect a foreign accent. He loves to hear our own true voice.

Sadly, most of us do not know our own voice. We've spent too many years with a noose around our necks, never having a good cry or a good belly laugh, never making funny or rude sounds the way we did in elementary school, never running through the fields and shouting at the top of our lungs. What would it take for us to cut loose? As a writer I poured myself for years into journals, volumes and volumes of them, until eventually I began to hear my own voice. I had to learn not to think so hard, but just to write. I had to notice what I was thinking when I wasn't thinking.

The Bible sums up contemplation in one verse: "Be still, and know that I am God" (Psalm 46:10). The knowing that takes place in this stillness is really beyond knowing. For contemplation is not just a remembering of God but a forgetting, a letting go of everything we thought we knew about Him in order to take hold of something new.

It is not that what we already knew was wrong, necessarily. But we must continually grasp the old truths in brand-new ways, and this means a bursting of the old forms. True learning does not consist in absorbing more and more facts, but in forging new pathways for comprehension. New discoveries are the product of new categories of thought, new ways of thinking. "The real voyage of discovery," wrote Marcel Proust, "consists not in seeking new landscapes but in having new eyes." We want a fresh newspaper every day, but how often do we change the way we read it?

Thus with God we come to know Him better only as we release Him from the box of our old thoughts. To know God is to find Him continually escaping all bounds. In stillness, we slip through the fences in our minds and hearts and escape to open country.

The strategy for knowing ourselves is the same. We must be still to know. The noise inside will keep us from knowing ourselves just as surely as it keeps us from praying. We must open the gate, forgetting ourselves, and forgetting everything we thought we knew about ourselves. Then we are ready for fresh knowledge, which, like food, is the best kind. To know ourselves, and others too, we must take a leap of trust and let people out of the box. Boxes are for the dead, not the living.

Reading Brother Lawrence, it's easy to get the impression that he thought about God all the time. In fact he thought about God very little. What he did was to experience God directly. For example, he liked to keep up a running conversation with God, just like a small child chattering away to his mother. To talk to God spontaneously, even in one's own mind, is both much harder and much easier than it sounds. It requires the elimination of the mental censor, the thought policeman who patrols and controls us into inertia. In this and in other ways, Brother Lawrence's practice of God's presence was different from thinking. In thinking, one is always a step removed from actual experience. But learning to chatter uninhibitedly to God is tantamount to quieting the mind completely.

Relaxing and letting go in solitude teaches us to take the same risk with people. If we want to know what to say in a conversation, for example, the best way is not to think about it. Why force language to be a rational activity? Practice people's presence nonverbally, and the verbal will take care of itself. Fire the thought police and learn to experience others directly, becoming available to them whole and uncensored. When you were five years old, your little friends knocked at the door to ask if you could come out to play. How do you answer this call today? Who stands now at your door and knocks? If you want to have fun, go out and play.

Firing the thought police is what I've had to do in order to write stimulating books. A lot of thinking goes into any book, but the actual writing must be spontaneous, like a good conversation. All creativity is like this. There is a time for brooding over the chaos, but there also comes a time for opening one's mouth and saying whatever comes out. When God said, "Let there be light!" He wasn't busy analyzing all the scientific properties of light. No, He was being spontaneous! No doubt He was as thrilled by the result as we are if we can stop thinking long enough to walk out in a field at dawn and let the morning break all over us as if sunlight had just that moment been created.

CHAPTER 20

Joy

*T*he children of God are called not only to a life of love, but to one of joy and peace in the Holy Spirit. We are to be "filled with an inexpressible and glorious joy" (1 Peter 1:8). Without such joy, we cannot really love. I have a friend who volunteered to work for a charitable organization that ministers to the poor, the sick, and the dying. He was turned down because, he was told, "The poor do not need depressed, neurotic people caring for them. They need people full of joy."

Why is Brother Lawrence so popular? One reason is his amazing joy! Who else testifies so brazenly, so preposterously, so infuriatingly to a continuous outpouring of joy day after day for thirty years? "I do not know what God wishes to do with me; I am always very happy," he writes sheepishly. "Everybody suffers and I who deserve the most severe punishments, I feel joys so continual and so great that I am scarcely able to contain them."⁴

How can this be? It doesn't seem fair, doesn't seem real. Yet we read Brother Lawrence because we, too, believe in joy, not only for him but for ourselves. We nurse a stubborn belief that somehow, someday, it might be possible to win through to a life of joy.

Isn't this precisely why vicissitudes frustrate us so? We fundamentally believe that happiness is like riding a bicycle, and that after a few spills and trials, anyone should be able to master it. When year after year goes by, and we still cannot get around the block without falling, perplexity sets in. We do not abandon belief in joy; we just cannot understand why it eludes us. Joy feels like it should be our birthright.

It is. "What has happened to all your joy?" Paul asked the Galatians (4:15). If we believe the gospel, it follows that we'll be happy about it too. Long-faced Christians can come up with all manner of sophisticated arguments against this simple truth. But if good news doesn't make a person happy, what will? Joy is the litmus test of true faith. We may not be able to comprehend our joy; like Brother Lawrence we may have to keep pinching ourselves. But joy indeed will be ours. It will be real and consistent, and its consistency will be a part of its reality.

Most of us think joy comes and goes. But in fact it is the nature of joy to be constant. The real thing is not a transitory mood, but a trait of character—if not of our own character, then certainly of the Holy Spirit's, who lives in us. His joy will be ours to the extent that we depend on Him rather than ourselves.

Joy is a fruit of the Holy Spirit. Flowers fade, and seeds may die without even taking root, but fruit is the mature, stable end product. The joy of the Holy Spirit within us is always ripe for the picking. Why then does joy seem so elusive? Only because we try to cling to it so tightly. The goal of Christian spirituality is not to feel good but to fight well. The moment we focus on good feelings, those feelings begin to slip away. We lose joy because we see it as a thing to be grasped rather than as a part of ourselves. If we held this treasure in our hearts rather than in our hands, we would know that it could not be taken away.

Being full of joy is like being full of breath. No one's lungs are constantly full, for it is necessary to exhale as well as to inhale. Nevertheless the supply of oxygen remains constant. Holding on to joy is like holding one's breath; the very act turns the joy stale. Why cling to one little lungful when a limitless supply is available? We are not going to suffocate any more than God is, whose breath is in and all around us. Knowing this, we are free to let go, to exhale, to feel all of our feelings as we have them, denying nothing.

The joyful Christian lives in a relaxed rhythm of breathing out and breathing in, giving and receiving love as needed. For joy and love are inseparable. We cannot experience the fullness of joy alone; true joy comes from deeply connecting with others. John begins one letter, "We write this to make our joy complete" (1 John 1:4) and ends another, "I hope to visit you and talk with you face to face, so that our joy may be complete" (2 John 12). Paul echoes, "Make my joy complete by being like-minded" (Philippians 2:2).

Fullness of joy comes from aligning ourselves with others. When an electrical circuit is completed, a light goes on or a motor hums. People are no more complicated than this. To be lit and humming, we must feel connected. In baseball a batter lines up a hurtling sphere with the sweet spot on his bat. The bat is designed for making this connection. In the same way you and I are designed to find the sweet spot in one another and to connect. Whenever we fulfill our purpose by making a good connection, the light of pure joy shines in our hearts.

CHAPTER 21

Embracing Suffering

*T*he other side of joy is suffering. To befriend ourselves we must embrace our lives wholly, including the suffering.

I used to shrink from suffering. Like many Christians I was in pursuit of a cross-less Christianity. Theologically I believed in the cross, but whenever pain touched my body or soul, I squealed like a stuck pig. Didn't Jesus suffer for me? Then why should I have to suffer too? Pain offended me; even a little could throw me into panic and doubt. When suffering went on (as it sometimes does) for days or weeks at a time, my faith collapsed.

From Brother Lawrence, I began to cherish the notion that it must be possible to be peaceful and happy at all times. If I wasn't, I felt something must be wrong. A little correction, a little adjustment to my walk of faith, and one day I would get it right.

However, I had overlooked one part of Brother Lawrence's teaching. It comes out most clearly later in his life, when he suffered increasingly from physical ills. "Love eases pain," he said then, "and when one loves God, one suffers for Him with joy and with courage."⁵ Again he wrote, "My pains and sufferings would be a paradise to me if I suffered them with God, and the greatest pleasures would be a hell if I enjoyed them without Him. All my solace is to suffer something for Him."[6]

From the New Testament on, all the great spiritual writers say the same. In true Christianity suffering is not something to avoid but to embrace gladly and even to desire. As Paul declared, "I want to know Christ and the power of his resurrection and the fellowship of sharing in his sufferings" (Philippians 3:10). Indeed we must "share in his sufferings in order that we may also share in his glory" (Romans 8:17).

When I resist suffering, all of my relationships—with God and myself and others—become shallow and unfulfilled. For if embraced, suffering can draw people together; otherwise it pushes them apart. When I suffer, I tend to judge myself, and so withdraw from others in insecurity. When others suffer, I tend to judge them, which again distances me. In either case the enemy is not the suffering itself, but the judgment.

Judgment is our strategy for keeping suffering at bay. But the fruit of judgment is the greatest suffering of all: alienation. What suffering could be worse than to be cut off from family, friends, and all the rich comfort of fellowship? Yet often we are so afraid of being hurt that we choose some measure of alienation rather than risk the pain of intimacy.

Whether we like it or not, we are going to share in the world's sufferings. Will our share of pain embitter us because we are unwilling to accept it? Or will we choose and even desire our sufferings, bearing them gladly because of the joy set before us?

Nothing is more damaging to our fellowship with Christ than

the rejection of suffering. We tend to be fair-weather friends of Jesus. We like His peace and joy and healing, but when He says He must suffer and die on the cross, we complain as Peter did, "Never, Lord!… This shall never happen to you!" (Matthew16:22). Peter was not worried about Jesus but about himself. All of us know instinctively that if our Lord goes to the cross, we too must go, for we are His followers.

Not only that, but we must share the suffering of everyone. Suffering is contagious, like a terrible disease. It is no idle fear that if we get too close to others their suffering might rub off on us. Because we are a part of one another, we cannot help but feel others' pain. Bearing these burdens, we enter into fellowship; avoiding them, we are alienated.

But don't we have enough pain of our own without taking on the pain of others? Herein lies a grand illusion, for there is no such thing as "pain of our own." The only private pain is the pain of isolation, which is hell. All other suffering is communal. Like love it can only be shared. If we are to share people's joys we must also share their sorrows. Shrinking from sorrow, we shrink from joy as well.

Therefore treat suffering as a friend; embrace it and it loses its sting. Brother Lawrence goes so far as to say, "I cannot understand how a soul that is with God and desires only Him can be capable of suffering; I have enough experience to believe this cannot be so."[7]

As we join the fellowship of suffering, the illusion of our separateness will fade away, swallowed up in the joy of being one with others.

CHAPTER 22

Mercy

*I*f you want to love yourself, become acquainted with mercy. "The quality of mercy is not strained," wrote Shakespeare, "but falleth as the gentle dew from heaven." Are you strained and stressed? Take lessons from the dew.

As my appetite for love has grown, I've noticed how often I scorn people in my heart, how easily I dismiss them as fools and write them off. For years this judgmentalism was so subtle that I wasn't aware of it. If my neighbor was having trouble at work, I'd think, *Well, he's in the wrong job anyway.* Or if someone I knew was in a car accident, out loud I might say, "Oh, how terrible!" but on the inside I'd mutter, *Well, it's about time that fellow had a comeuppance. You can't live in the fast lane forever.*

In short, though I begged God for mercy for myself, I had no real mercy for others. Inwardly I was glad when they got what they deserved. I wasn't ready to live in the kingdom of God; I wanted to live with a black-and-white rule book. When my brothers and sisters got their hands slapped, I smiled at the justice of it. When my own hands got slapped, I squealed with outrage.

If you want mercy, show mercy. "What does the LORD require of you? To act justly and to love mercy and to walk humbly with your God" (Micah 6:8). Mercy is the bridge between suffering and joy. Showing mercy to yourself will mitigate your suffering. Showing mercy to others brings joy.

"Rejoice in the Lord always," exhorts Paul, but in the next breath he says, "Let your gentleness be evident to all" (Philippians 4:4-5). Gentle mercy is the necessary companion of joy. Joy wants the whole world to rejoice with it, but mercy understands the reasons why others cannot be happy right now. Mercy understands these reasons so deeply that it embraces them as its own, refusing to separate itself in any way from the unhappy, the embittered, the angry, the worldly. Rather than remaining aloof from such people, mercy, without diminishing its own light, joins them in their dark place.

Mercy sides with people even when they are wrong, as Jesus did. Satan is an accuser, but Jesus is our advocate. Satan kicks us when we're down, but Jesus gets down beside us to absorb the kicks. In the ancient dispute between God and man, Jesus takes God's side, but He also takes man's side. In fact when push came to shove on Calvary, Jesus by the will of God took our side, though we were plainly in the wrong. "God demonstrates his own love for us in this: While we were still sinners, Christ died for us" (Romans 5:8).

Mercy sides with people. Christians can get all hot and bothered about what other people believe. But mercy is less interested in what people believe than in why. Many unbelievers have good reasons for their unbelief. Looking for the *whys* of belief instead of the *whats* helps us to love people rather than to judge them.

"Mercy triumphs over judgment" (James 2:13) because mercy is more interested in maintaining relationships than in being right. Mercy is the glue of friendship. Glue is what is needed in broken places. Friends are initially attracted by the good they see in one another. But mercy is what happens when we see the bad in our friends and remain attracted. The bad is not itself attractive, but neither is it repulsive. Mercy neutralizes sin in much the way that a surgeon anesthetizes a patient in order to operate. To the merciful, evil is no threat but rather a kind of tragic hollowness that mercy longs to fill.

"God made [Christ] who had no sin to be sin for us" (2 Corinthians 5:21). As ugly as sin is, Christ did not shrink from taking it on. Instead He moved toward it and donned it like a familiar coat. The cross was a kind of second incarnation of Christ. In the first incarnation God took on human nature; in the second He took on fallen human nature. In doing so He became like all the rest of us and died.

In the face of this astounding example of God's identification with humanity, what reason is left us to separate ourselves in any way from other people, however ugly, however wrong, however bad they may be? No, there is nothing that mercy cannot comprehend, nowhere so dark that mercy will not go. Mercy is the oil in the lamp of joy. It is the part of us that burns so that our light may shine.

CHAPTER 23

Sadness

*I*f you love yourself, you'll feel your feelings—all of them. Most people can identify their stronger feelings, such as anger or fear. But as you make contact with the real you, subtler and deeper feelings will arise. One of the deepest of all is sadness. For underneath anger is fear, and underneath fear is sadness.

When you are angry, ask yourself what you are afraid of. Leave the anger and get to the fear underneath. Be courageous enough to encounter the naked fear without covering it up with anger. Then, when you are good and tired of being afraid, ask yourself what sadness underlies the fear. Get in touch with your deep sadness; feel it and you will be free. Anger and fear both resist the gospel of love and freedom. But sadness opens the heart's door.

Sadness is one of the Beatitudes: "Blessed [or in some translations, "Happy"] are those who mourn, for they will be comforted" (Matthew 5:4). This suggests that sadness is very, very close to happiness. One could almost say that to the Christian they are the same—or at least that there is no true happiness without its wistful tint of divine sadness, and no sadness that does not stand on the doorstep of happiness.

Sadness keeps happiness practical. Sadness makes happiness soft and pliable. There is a hard-edged happiness that charges headlong into the world and is quickly depleted. But no emotion is more enduring than happiness muted with the pastel pragmatism of sadness. How can we not be sad with the world the way it is? How can we not be happy with God as faithful and true as He is!

So sadness and happiness go together. Together they make a pure heart. When we hear the word *purity*, perhaps we think of one single thing, simple and undiluted. But whenever we reduce the Christian life to one thing—whether it be freedom, joy, victory, or even love—we fall into error. If even love could stand alone, what use would there be for hope and faith?

No, true purity is not one thing but a balanced mix of godly virtues. Hence Peter advises, "Make every effort to add to your faith goodness; and to goodness, knowledge; and to knowledge, self-control" and so on (2 Peter 1:5-7). In the same way, to happiness add sadness, and to sadness, happiness. These two are good companions, strong friends. Don't take your feelings straight; mix them in healthy proportions. Our road is long, and we need to take another's hand and travel together. Whatever you are feeling—whether frustrated, fearful, or happy—take the hand of sadness, and it will not disappoint you.

Often sadness brings us close to other people, especially in their pain. Gladness is not always a good bridge to a troubled world. Sadness is sturdier stuff and can better bear the weight of two. In relationships, sadness is sturdy precisely because of its instability, its intrinsic uncertainty. No doubt this is why we avoid it so strenuously, for in sadness longings rise to the surface that we cannot fulfill by ourselves, but only through dependence on others. Sadness is trustworthy because it places no stock in itself. Happiness can be cocky, but not sadness. Inherently humble, sadness knows it is nothing in itself.

Sadness signals change. It is an intermediate emotion, a feeling that is going somewhere. Like a seventh or a ninth chord in music, it is rich in subtle tones that tend toward resolution, lean toward home. This is what distinguishes sadness from moroseness, self-pity, or depression, all of which have a feeling of stuckness. Sadness is always in motion in the backfield. You will know the real thing by this sense of movement toward happiness. In photographs, crying and laughing are hard to tell apart.

Sadness is like that moment in a rainstorm when the rain has not yet stopped, but there is a perceptible brightening, and there comes that subtle change in the atmosphere signifying the imminence of a rainbow. Sadness is hopeful. Anger feels hard in the body, fear feels alien, and depression is like a dull poison. But sadness is at home in flesh and blood. It is a soft and relaxed presence, a comfortable garment for the heart.

Sadness is linked to the biblical idea of repentance. Repentance sounds like something we do not want to do. "Repent, for the kingdom of God is at hand" may suggest, "Oh no! God is about to clobber me, and I better get pious real quick." But that is not the idea at all. The message to repent is more an announcement than a warning.

It is a proclamation of such great, great joy on the way, that preparations are in order. The joy is not here yet, but it is coming. Sadness births dreams. How better to prepare for joy than by softening, gentling, tenderizing the heart with sadness? This is the mood of repentance. It feels like relief, not a burden. It is what happens when the heart is changing.

Sadness may even be worth hanging on to, prolonging a little, because in itself it feels so good and is so real. We can easily get the wrong idea about love and think we are doing it when we are not. But sadness is honest. In its dark, rich, fertile soil, everything good grows. Therefore cultivate sadness. Seek a happy, lighthearted life, and it will elude you. But seek a godly sadness, and happiness will come running as if its name had been called.

Happy are those who mourn. Who are we to mourn for? First of all for ourselves. "Daughters of Jerusalem, do not weep for me," said Jesus on His way to the cross; "weep for yourselves and for your children" (Luke 23:28). Most of us treat ourselves badly. Intensely critical of our failings, we punish ourselves by getting frustrated and angry, or else we quiver in anxiety, self-consciousness, and fear. But when do we ever simply mourn? When do we lay aside the anger and the fear and get down to the bedrock of sadness?

Mourning seems to be the last thing we come to. After we have worried, beaten ourselves up, heaped high inner abuse, prodded and kicked ourselves like starved and exhausted beasts of burden, and finally smoldered in bitter despair—what is left? Mourning. If we can simply be sad, there is hope. Sadness is the appropriate response to looking our poor, miserable selves square in the eye, denying nothing yet refusing to condemn. Sadness is the sign that we are finally giving up on trying to atone for our own sin. Sadness is the beginning of mercy. We cannot be merciful toward others until we become tender with ourselves.

In relationships, sadness is compassion. In sadness there is no harshness, no reproach or sullen suspicion. Sadness does not boast, perform, or manipulate. All that is washed away, leaving a humble, tender respect for even the worst of sinners, beginning with oneself.

Sadness works against sin. What else are you going to do with sin, either your own or your neighbor's? You cannot love it, nor can you ever quite stamp it out. Therefore, be sad. Mourn and you will be comforted.

CHAPTER 24

Living with Chaos

One day when my wife asked me cheerily how I was, I hung my head and moaned, "Oh, Karen, I'm so mixed up today."

"Well then," she responded brightly, "why don't you just decide to have a mixed-up day?"

At first I resented this cocky advice. But, as so often happens, I found myself pondering what she'd said. And five minutes later a sloppy smile spread across my face and stayed there the rest of the day.

Karen was right: One day does not a chaos make. There was no need for me to be overwhelmed by confusion. Every day is different. There were six days of creation, and each day had its own peculiar character. One day was for separating light from darkness; that's all that happened. On another day all the plants were created, and another day was set aside for animals. Some days were very basic: preparing the canvas and brushing on the background wash. Other days were filled with complex detail.

If this is the way God's days are, each one with its unique tone and pace, will it not be the same for us? Shouldn't we seek to be sensitive each morning to the flavor of the day before us? If a day is for brooding, and I rush into it eager for action, there's going to be a collision. If yesterday was full of joy, I may be in for an unpleasant surprise if I expect today to be the same. Expectations could be defined as "premeditated resentments." Better to start each day with a clean slate and be ready for whatever comes.

In a recent week of mine, one day was devoted to solving problems in a friendship. The next day I felt filled with energy and was able to do scads of work. The following day had a more somber demeanor, as I found myself repenting for energy misspent. Then I had a day of mystery in which I could not understand anything. Next came a day in which, having abandoned rational thought, I found deep comfort in purely physical things: a tree outside my window, the way the wind moved through it, the feel of my wife's hair. The next day arrived with a burst of creativity and I jotted down all kinds of new ideas for this book. And then came a day of rampant pride and foolishness. And so it goes.

My days are not the same. No two are the same. How about yours? Do you listen for the mood of each day and live accordingly? Or do you arm yourself against reality with expectations and agendas? Each of the days just described was filled with many shades and turnings of mood. Yet each one also had a predominant character that could almost be summed up in a single word. Moreover, each day had its entry point, a point at which it could be identified and received for what it was or else missed like a departing train.

Have you room in your life for a mixed-up day? If not, it may be because you see *yourself* as being mixed up rather than your day, and this terrifies you. How readily we fall into this trap! We have strong negative feelings, and we identify with those feelings rather than stand apart in a safe place until the confusion has passed. The Bible describes God as a "rock" and a "refuge": "God is our refuge and strength, an ever-present help in trouble" (Psalm 46:1). The Lord resides in that strong, quiet place deep within, and it is no shame to hide ourselves there.

Try looking at it this way: If I experience mixed-up feelings, it is because in the center of my being a principle of order is at work, exploring, questioning, probing for terra firma. This, it turns out, is exactly how God Himself operates: "Now the earth was formless and empty, darkness was over the surface of the deep, and the Spirit of God was hovering over the waters" (Genesis 1:2). Without divine brooding, there would have been no creation.

God never wanted a clockwork universe. He wanted us to experience excitement and surprise, and so He created mystery, freedom, luck, and limitless possibility. "Deep in the human unconscious," writes Frank Herbert, "is a pervasive need for a logical universe that makes sense. But the real universe is always one step beyond logic."

God is not merely a logician but an artist and a lover. Maybe He sat down with pencil and paper and deliberately designed every single snowflake. But maybe He just tossed a big bag of confetti in the air and it came out the way it did just because of who He is!

If this is God's nature—always beyond logic—then it's no wonder you and I have our mixed-up days. To be human is to be poised always on the brink of chaos, plunging forward moment by moment into the unknown, the unformed. Each one of us shares the famous motto of the starship *Enterprise*—"to boldly go where no man has gone before."

It helps to know this about ourselves. If part of my job as a human being is to eat chaos for breakfast, then maybe I don't have to feel so bad about failing so much. Maybe I can cut myself some slack, allow myself a certain amount of tension, trouble, and plain stupidity without always shouldering the blame. This is not who I am, this malfunctioning misfit, this bumbling bucket of bolts. No, the fog I live in is just the chaos I'm pushing through, scrambling to create order as I go. Like Paul I am "hard pressed on every side, but not crushed; perplexed, but not in despair;...struck down, but not destroyed" (2 Corinthians 4:8-9).

Chaos is the active ingredient in the world; it's the yeast in the dough. It's the mixed-up things, the things that don't fit or make sense, that bring us news of reality.

CHAPTER 25

Fun

As we learn to live with chaos, we can start having fun with life. Good clean fun holds tremendous spiritual power. Fresh, spontaneous, natural, renewing—fun restores us to our true selves.

One of my favorite cartoons shows two robed men, obviously guru and disciple, sitting cross-legged outside a cave on a mountaintop. The guru wears a blissful smile as the other says incredulously, "The hokey-pokey? *That's* what it's all about?"

Yes, putting your whole self in is what life is all about. Fun is participatory. You cannot have fun standing on the sidelines. You must join in the game. Do a little shaking and turn yourself about, and see what happens. Fun cannot be planned. It has to happen. To have fun happen to you, be a happening person. Are you a stick-in-the-mud or are you still happening?

Brother Lawrence was a fun-lover who confessed that the joy of the Lord so overwhelmed him at times that he would "cry out, singing and dancing like a madman."[8] We're told that "for almost thirty years his soul was filled with interior joys so continual and sometimes so great that to contain them and prevent their outward manifestation, he had to resort to behavior that seemed more fool-ishness than piety."[9]

What a shame that Brother Lawrence apparently had no one with whom to share this holy fun, and so felt he had to restrain it. His monastery, like many religious institutions, must have been pretty straitlaced. Why is it that pure fun is so rare a visitor to church? Perhaps it's because fun is difficult to fake. Piety, good behav-ior, even mercy and love may be closely rendered by facsimiles. But fun, to the person having it, does not lie. Either it's the real thing or it isn't. You're either having fun or you're not, and only you know the difference.

Colin Goode and Costas Criticos are the best of friends. For years now they have lived thousands of miles apart, yet neither time nor distance has dimmed the quality of their friendship. I once asked Colin what makes this friendship so rich. What is it about Costas that he likes? Colin's face lit up, and without a moment's hesitation he replied: "We have fun together! Whenever I'm with Costas we have such a good time. The last time I saw him, we happened to pass the hat counter in a department store, and we couldn't resist pausing to try on a few hats. Before long we were laughing and posing and making faces, having the most hilarious time just horsing around. That's the way it always is with Costas and me. We laugh and laugh, and it washes all the bad out of me."

Plato wrote, "You can learn more about a man in an hour of play than in a year of conversation." Play is essentially free exploration of the world. It's how children learn. The enemy of play is fear. When we're fearful, we stop experimenting and so we stop learning and growing. What are we so afraid of? Mostly, we're afraid of looking foolish. What if we make a mistake? But mistakes are the essence of experiment. We're going to make mistakes anyway. Make them freely and plentifully, and our progress will be all the quicker. We should make so many mistakes every day that they do not matter anymore. In real foolishness there is no such thing as error, for there is no right way. A fool, like a Christian, lives beyond the law.

How tragic that the very thing that could set us free—playing the fool—is the thing we will not do. When we're afraid to be fools, we end up being afraid to be anything. It becomes easier just to disappear, to fade into the woodwork. We get to thinking that righteousness means hiding our faults, when really the truth is just the opposite. Pride wants to look good, but humility has no fear of looking bad. People will see our faults anyway; like Paul, we should glory in our weaknesses. Then we'll be free to have fun.

I'd like to make a film of a hundred children at the point when they realize that it is not okay to do certain things in public. I fancy this is the moment when people lose touch with the best playmate they'll ever have, their own inner child.

Are you still friends with the little girl or the little boy inside? If not, you won't make friends with anyone else either. Other kids will come calling, but you won't be home.

Be home to the child you still are at heart. He or she is your ticket to having fun.

CHAPTER 26

The Laughing Place

One night, on the eve of my birthday, I woke up laughing from a dream. I was laughing so hard that I woke my wife, too, who was alarmed because she thought I was crying! In my dream I was with a group of children at a birthday party. The party had progressed to the point where the cake was about to be cut. But suddenly an argument erupted over who would get the biggest piece, and whether there was enough cake to go around. Finally the first piece was cut and served, and when I looked at it sitting there on the plate, I burst out laughing.

What struck my funny bone was that this one piece of cake was so enormous! It was far more than any one person could eat. It was a scrumptious chocolate angel food cake in two layers, and I saw clearly that even if this one piece were cut in two along the center filling, still either half would be too much for even the heartiest appetite. Moreover I realized that each child would receive a piece of cake this big.

How hilarious! Here we had just been fretting and fighting over the cake being too small, when there was enough cake to sink a ship.

That's why I woke up in the middle of the night, laughing until my chin was wet with tears. Instead of arguing, we kids should have saved our energy for stuffing our faces.

Reflecting on the meaning of this dream, I saw that all of us, regardless of our lot in life, receive a piece of cake this big. Not only is it too big for you alone, but even if you were to cut it in two and share it, still you would have too much. What is this piece of cake that, when you see it for what it is, banishes anxiety and strife and fills you with hilarity?

It's you! Not the old you of whom you're sick to death, but the new you whose life is in Christ. Do you live with the chronic fear that there's not enough of you to go around? But there is! There's more than enough, for "we are more than conquerors through him who loved us" (Romans 8:37). If only we could open our eyes to see the size of our portion, wouldn't we wake from our anxious dream and burst out laughing? "When the LORD brought back the captives to Zion, we were like men who dreamed. Our mouths were filled with laughter, our tongues with songs of joy" (Psalm 126:1-2).

Great, deep laughter erupts when you glimpse the whole truth of who you are. The laughter is a kind of explosion, as if the lid had just blown off your head because the truth is too large for you to contain, to comprehend, or even to believe for long. You believe it while you're laughing, but soon after, the lid goes back on. Why? Because you like to pretend that you are smaller-than-life. Being larger-than-life is scary, because if it's true, you have nothing left to be afraid of, nothing to complain about, no more reason to be miserable.

At California's Disneyland, one the most popular rides is called Splash Mountain. A water ride, it propels passengers in small log-boats through a narrow sluiceway. Darkness, ups and downs, varying speeds, zesty music, and a cast of bizarre Disney characters all combine to fill the ride with surprises. The atmosphere is enchanting, delightful, refreshing, fun. At least, until you get to the end.

Upon entering one of the final chambers, suddenly the whole tone of the ride changes. Where formerly the song was "Zippity-Do-Dah," there now begins a mournful dirge. Foreboding characters chant of woe and death. One of these, a mangy black buzzard perched on a rafter just above your head, cocks a glazed eye and warns you in a mocking croak, "Everybody has a laughing place."

This happens just as your floating log-boat is being hauled up a long, steep incline. Since what goes up must come down, you have a good idea of what's ahead. The darkness, the chilling music, the grinding clank of the machinery—it all gets to you. You begin to sense that this "laughing place," whatever it is, must be a mighty scary business. And so it is.

The first time I rode Splash Mountain, I was so charmed by the overall effect that I felt no fear. Indeed what I discovered beyond that final high watery hill really did make me yell and laugh aloud with pleasure. I was too surprised, I suppose, to be scared.

However, the second time I experienced this ride was a different story. Feeling out of sorts that day, I was in no mood to squeal with joy. I was hoping the ride might snap me out of my bleakness, but instead it terrified me. What was I so afraid of? Certainly not a little plunge on a roller-coaster ride. No, what frightened me was the feeling of being smaller-than-life. I was trying to be free, but trying is lying.

That old buzzard was right: Everybody *does* have a laughing

place. The only problem is our fear of going there. Finding t[
ing place is a scary business, because once we do find it—once we
wake up in the night and laugh out loud at how monstrous that slab
of cake really is—after this, what excuse do we have anymore to be
gloomy? Once and for all the rug has been pulled out from under us,
and we've discovered that standing on thin air is not really so bad.
Like Peter, at one time or another we have all stepped out of our boat
and walked on the water. Why don't we just keep on going?

Nelson Mandela, having spent the best years of his life in a South
African prison, emerged to become the president of his country. In
his inauguration speech he quoted these words: "Our deepest fear is
not that we are inadequate. Our deepest fear is that we are powerful
beyond measure. It is our light, not our darkness, that most frightens
us. We ask ourselves, who am I to be brilliant, gorgeous, talented and
fabulous? Actually, who are you *not* to be? You are a child of God.
Your playing small doesn't serve the world. There's nothing enlight-
ened about shrinking so that other people won't feel insecure around
you. We were born to manifest the glory of God that is within us. It's
not just in some of us; it's in everyone. And as we let our own light
shine, we unconsciously give other people permission to do the same.
As we are liberated from our own fear, our presence automatically
liberates others."[10]

PRESENCE

There is no way of telling people that they are
all walking around shining like the sun.

THOMAS MERTON

The night before I began writing this book, my friend Niel Pearce phoned to tell me of a wonderful experience he'd had. Niel is a teacher, and one night he met two of his students at the movie theater. Seeing him before the show, the two boys greeted him with, "Hello, Mr. Pearce." Later on, coming out of the theater, they said, "Good-bye, Mr. Pearce."

That was all that happened.

And yet, Niel said, there seemed such tenderness in the way those boys spoke to him, such warmth and light in their eyes and faces and such a holy innocence in their whole bearing, that he was deeply moved. Though this incident had happened several days before, he was still pondering it.

"I don't know what to call this, Mike," he told me. "But it strikes me that what I saw in those two boys, whatever it is, is vastly more important than any amount of money, than fame or any other goal we might seek, or than all the power of all the governments in the world."

Simple as this story is, just hearing it touched me in the same deep way it had Niel. Immediately I thought, *Yes, that's what I want to get at in my book. I want people to wake up to the wonder of simply being in one another's presence.*

I use this word *presence* not only because Brother Lawrence used it, but because he got it from the Bible. Throughout Scripture the word is used commonly both of God and of people. The King of heaven has a presence (2 Chronicles 20:9), and so do the kings of earth (Esther 1:16), as do all people (Psalm 116:14). Moses "entered the LORD's presence to speak with him" (Exodus 34:34), and it seems to me that we must do the same with one another. To understand people, to know them, to enjoy them, we must humble ourselves and enter their presence.

To enter the presence of people is to allow others to be more special, more noticeable or present than we are to ourselves. When this happened to Niel Pearce outside the theater one evening, it came as an unexpected gift. But a gift can be developed and mined. The initial experience is just the first gleam of the mother lode.

Obviously there was a mystical dimension to Niel's experience, yet at the same time it could not have been more natural. Isn't perfect naturalness the hallmark of true mysticism? What happened to Niel could happen to you in the supermarket, on an airplane, or while leafing through a *People* magazine. In this lonely world, anyone, anywhere can be suddenly, strangely moved by the mere presence—miraculous in and of itself—of another human being.

I am convinced that this experience comes to all of us quite commonly, only we tend not to treasure it as Niel did. At the birth of Jesus, Mary "treasured up all these things and pondered them in her heart" (Luke 2:19). Don't most mothers do the same? To be sure, Jesus was a unique child, but didn't He come into the world to show us that everyone is unique, that everyone can become God's child? Why don't we treasure God's children as He does?

One reason we do not treasure people is that they are so common, and another reason is that they are so bad. Rather than leave it to God to judge people's badness, we do it ourselves by writing others off and shouldering them aside. As for being common, we are common stuff ourselves, which is why we have to work so hard on our self-image. Wouldn't it be easier just to cherish one another?

My friend Norman Oldham tells of encountering a young man in a department store. Something about this fellow touched Norman's heart. Though no words were exchanged, he had a quality of purity, innocence, and light that left Norman feeling brushed by glory.

So striking was this experience that Norman wonders whether the young man might have been an angel. In any case, it doesn't take an angel to deliver a heaven-sent message. What if we were to open our eyes to see, in the ordinary people we meet all around us every day, the messages of heaven?

CHAPTER 27

Self-Absorption

*A*ir travel is, to me, an opportunity for silent retreat. There above the clouds, I like to take the entire flight for thinking, resting, praying, gazing out the window, and generally making the most of this amazing provision of a hideaway in the sky. The moment the plane leaves the runway, all my problems fall away as if a multitude of invisible cords had been cut, and for a few hours I float free of earthly care. As for the in-flight movie, the magazines, and the person beside me, these all present equal potential for distraction, and I'm good at shutting them out.

On one journey, however, I sat beside a young man in his midtwenties. I was in a rare mood, and I found myself not only striking up a conversation with him but enjoying it. He began by being curious about my work, and since I love what I do, I was happy to paint for him a glowing picture of the glories of the writing life. I also drew him out on his interests, and from there the talk went deeper.

It was one of those conversations that there is no stopping;

everything we touched on led to something more, like going from room to room in an intriguing old mansion. Normally shy and guarded, I surprised myself by being voluble, witty, engaging, and entertaining. We talked most of the way from Vancouver to Toronto.

However, just moments after we had parted company at the Toronto airport, I felt strangely relieved. Something about our encounter, it seemed, was not quite right. On reflection I realized that I had created the illusion of relationship, not the real thing. Although we had broached some deep and intimate subjects, it was no more than what happened all the time in airplanes, coffee shops, and countless bars across the country, where people gave their best energies to being interesting for strangers without ever really shedding their loneliness.

What was the problem? It dawned on me that as much as I had enjoyed our conversation, it was not the young man I had enjoyed so much as my own charm and conviviality. I'd been absorbed in being interesting without truly being interested. What I had enjoyed was not him but my own enjoyment of him.

Isn't this the same trap we fall into with God? How easily we convince ourselves that we are praying to the Lord when in reality we are locked in our own thoughts. We need to ask: If I'm happy, am I really rejoicing in Him, or am I rejoicing in my own self-satisfaction? If I'm worried or afraid, am I truly and humbly asking Him for help, or is my mind busy trying to work out some plan (however spiritual it may seem) for getting myself out of trouble?

There is a difference between God's presence and His presents. Brother Lawrence, aware of this subtle distinction, made a decision "to do everything for the love of God, seeking Him alone and nothing else, not even His gifts." He found that "this behavior of his soul caused God to grant him endless graces."[1]

When it comes to people, do you want their presents or their presence? My experience on the plane showed me graphically that it is possible to have a good time with someone without actually being with that person. I can *enjoy myself,* as the expression goes, without actually enjoying anyone else. The result is not fellowship but self-absorption. Other people can tell the difference. While it may be entertaining to be with a colorful extrovert, we all know the feeling of being lost in the dust of someone else's exuberant sociability.

Unlike self-love, which frees one to love others, self-absorption keeps one trapped in isolation. As simplistic as it sounds, the antidote to self-absorption is the practice of the real presence of God and of people. If God and others were not real persons, this would not work. But because they are real, we can have the transcendent experience of entering their presence.

CHAPTER 28

Entering
the Presence

How often we struggle to understand God without entering His presence! This never works with God, and it never works with people.

What happens when we enter the Lord's presence? Psalm 73:16-17 puts it this way:

> When I tried to understand all this,
> it was oppressive to me
> till I entered the sanctuary of God;
> then I understood.

When bringing some problem or question to the Lord, I find He seldom answers me directly. Instead He just wants to be with me, to enjoy my company, and He hopes I too will enjoy Him. In this mutual enjoyment, my problems and questions begin to dissolve.

They do not disappear, exactly, but their hold on my mind loosens. Problems change shape, and questions turn into mysteries.

While I always receive answers to my prayers, they seldom come in the way I expect. Often I realize that I have been asking the wrong question, or that I have not really been asking at all, but rather seeking endorsement for an answer of my own devising. True asking is a humbling experience. It begins with the frank admission, "I do not know," and with the sincere belief that there is One who does know. To ask honestly, I must let go of all predetermined answers and relax enough with the Lord of the universe to enter into His awesome and delightful presence.

How else to say this? Try reading the following verses. Read them aloud:

> Within your temple, O God,
>> we meditate on your unfailing love.
> Like your name, O God,
>> your praise reaches to the ends of the earth;
>> your right hand is filled with righteousness.
> (Psalm 48:9-10)

Now ask yourself: Did you say these words to God? That's who they're addressed to. Did you say them to Him or to yourself? Don't lie. You know the difference. Now read the verses again, this time deliberately addressing them to God.

Many people say they cannot feel God's presence. But if you honestly say these words to God, you will feel something. If you think you feel nothing, then ask yourself, "What was I feeling when

I felt nothing? What happened when nothing happened?" Be honest. Find a way to outwit your natural state of blockheaded torpor. Perhaps you pride yourself on being orthodox (a word that means "having right doctrine"), but are you *orthopathic* ("having right feelings")?

If you seek God with all your heart, you will feel something. You cannot help it, because God is real. The only reason you would not feel something is if you are playing some game to keep God at bay. Only draw near to God, and He will draw near to you. Talk to God as if He is real, and He will be. Suddenly you will be outside the wire cage of your mind, reaching out to God, and something is bound to happen, because the Lord is faithful and good and He will not fail to respond to you.

People, it is true, are not always faithful and good. Nevertheless, they too are real. They have a real presence. You can remove the veil and become aware of others and address yourself directly to them. Why not try it? Something is bound to happen. You might find yourself having a lively conversation. You may even make a friend. At the very least, perhaps you'll see something about another person that you never saw before When you give someone your attention, you may or may not have the favor returned. Others might not give you their attention, but this part doesn't matter. What matters is that you do your part. Practice someone's presence, and you yourself will be more alive. You will know when you are doing it because you will feel the difference.

CHAPTER 29

Living in the Present

The word *presence* is rich in connotation. Just as the word *present* means both *here* and *now*, so the word *presence* evokes a double sense of hereness and nowness. When Brother Lawrence practiced God's presence, he was not interested in any other place except the one where he was, nor in any other time except the present, nor in any other business or task except the one at hand. He knew that God is always present; the problem is that we are not. In our minds we tend to live more in the past and the future than in the present, and so our bodies too get tricked into thinking they are not quite here, not fully alive.

Daydreaming, of course, is not without value. Through imagination and reflection our minds become a theater where we can experiment with different strategies for living. But the trap is that we can devote more energy to fantasizing than to actually living life. If we wish to be with God, we must meet Him in the here and now. The Lord's name, I AM (Exodus 3:14), tells how we are to relate to Him. Yesterday's discouragement need not hold us back from victory today. Similarly, yesterday's miracle may not help at all in facing today's obstacle. However grateful I may have been to be alive yesterday, it means nothing if I wake up grumpy this morning. I need to be thankful *now*. I need a fresh touch of awe right now. Sufficient unto the day is the evil thereof, and the good, too. There is manna aplenty for every moment.

Each day as I come before God I ask not, "What *should* be happening in my life?" but rather, "What *is* happening?" I say, "Lord, what are You up to right now? What is Your gift for me today?" While it's important to rehearse all the wonderful ways that God has met me in the past, the question is, *Where am I with God right now?* Each day, each moment, is a field of fresh fallen snow unbroken by any footstep. In this present moment, even as I wash these dishes, chat with this neighbor, or read this book—am I in God's presence? What good is it to have been in God's presence this morning if I am not now? Eternal life is lived in the present. What is keeping me right now from being fully present to myself, to my friend, and to my God?

When the Lord revealed His name as I AM, He gave us the most powerful weapon against every form of deception. This name banishes all fear, since fear has to do with what has happened in the past or what may happen in the future. This name is the instrument of forgiveness, for it wipes clean the criminal record of even the worst offender. This name is the key that ushers God into any and every circumstance no matter how bleak. This name creates miracles, for "Jesus Christ is the same yesterday and today and forever" (Hebrews 13:8). Do we use this name? When we call upon God, do we bemoan His absence, or do we practice His presence, His hereness and nowness?

Love is like oxygen. The breath of it I had just a moment ago will do me no good if I do not take another breath soon. To stay alive I must keep breathing. In both Greek and Hebrew the word for *breath* is the same as the word for *spirit*. But there is one vital difference between physical and spiritual breathing, for while the former is governed by an autonomic system, the latter is governed by the will. Spiritually each breath is different from the last, and for this reason spiritual growth cannot happen automatically but only through conscious choice. This means that the spiritual life by its very nature is experimental, a matter of trial and error.

Experimentation is what keeps spirituality in the here and now. It's what keeps relationships fresh and vital. Getting to know someone, whether it is God or a human being, cannot happen without trial and error. Fear of error is a sure recipe for stagnation. If you do what you always do, you'll get what you always get. Why not try something different? Experimentation brings relationships into the present moment where they must be in order to change and grow.

Agnes Sanford suggests making experiments in prayer. Many of us, she writes, do not receive answers to our prayers because we give up and lose faith too easily. For example, if our initial prayers for healing do not work, we assume that God does not want to heal. It never occurs to us that if one sort of prayer fails, we might try a different tack and keep on trying until we learn what pleases God and how to release His power. We needn't grow discouraged in this process; it is a matter of accepting the experimental nature of a vibrant relationship.[2]

Vital relationships with people always have an experimental edge. When a foundation of trust is in place, there is no fear of doing things differently. The fear, rather, is of too much sameness and predictability. Do people keep us on our toes, keep us guessing? Good! This means we can approach each person with a sense of expectation, a readiness for discovery, a crisp freshness, a lively spontaneity. These will be the signs and proofs that we are living in the presence of people.

CHAPTER 30

God in People

One day I was walking with my wife in a cemetery. At one point I stood wrapped in thought under a tree while Karen went off to inspect a particular grave. Watching her from a distance, I found myself imagining it was my grave she was visiting. In that one snapshot all the tender love of our married life flashed before me. In the next frame I pictured myself, years hence, visiting her grave. Still lost in this reverie, I looked up suddenly to see Karen, very much alive, walking toward me. You can imagine how vibrant and resplendent with light she appeared! It was just as if she had risen from the grave to be reunited with me!

You never know when the phenomenon of a person's presence might jump up and surprise you. If you aren't on the lookout, you may miss it. You have to be ready for it, train for it. A poet can be feeling flat one moment and the next be writing away furiously. So it is with people: You never know when one of them may hand you a great line. It's worth it to remain open. It's worthwhile paying attention to everyone and everything. If what people are saying does not interest you, become interested in what they are not saying. Be the sort of person who, when some bore is talking your ear off, happens to notice the peculiar spot of light shining like a jewel in his hair.

If people bore you, doesn't it really mean you are bored with yourself? We wish people would change and become interesting, but often they cannot because we will not let them. We blame others when really it is we who refuse to be people around whom others can breathe easily and let themselves go. If you want to practice people's presence, start by giving your own. Become present to others. Be the first one on your block to give your neighbors the gift of your true self.

You do not have to feel good to practice people's presence any more than you have to feel good to pray. What if you didn't have to worry anymore about how you felt in public? What if feeling bad only left more room to be surprised? Don't let your moods keep you isolated from people. The darkest of nights is the best time to view the stars. Wasn't it dark the night you first opened your heart to Jesus? In the same way, ask people into your life. Our churches are full of born-again believers who have never opened their hearts to one another.

We are to love our neighbor as ourself because our neighbor is included in ourself. Where do I leave off and where does my neighbor begin? There is no telling, for we are a part of one another. If Christ is in me, then the people who make up His body are also in me. We are members of one another.

We can see something of God in each person, and we see Him especially in all His people put together—that is, in the church. The church is the body of Christ, His hands and feet and heart, the part of Him that is manifest in the world. Looking out over the congregation one Sunday morning, my pastor Bob Rose said, "If you want an idea of what God looks like, He looks like us." John meant much the same when he wrote, "No one has ever seen God; but if we love one another, God lives in us" (1 John 4:12). The divine is discovered in the personal, the absolute in the particular.

The church is God's family album. Each member is a snapshot of the Creator of the universe. Each image is unique: a different angle, a different mood, a different moment in the life of God. Here He is as a tiny baby. Here He is as an old man. Here is a beautiful woman who doesn't even realize her own beauty, who doesn't see in herself the beauty of God. And here is a young man so confused that he is hardly aware of God living in him. Why not become aware for him?

Be a camera. Empty yourself and take pictures of people. Let yourself be surprised. Open your shutter just for a moment, and be amazed at the illumination that floods in. Even though you've already encountered millions of people in your lifetime, let this one, the one in front of you right now, astonish you.

CHAPTER 31

Looking

There are many ways of looking at people, many ways of using our eyes. We are aware of the problem of "not knowing what to do with our hands," but the same problem crops up with eyes. Where to look? What to do with our eyes during conversation? Keep them roving, looking mostly away from the other, but now and then stealing a glance or even braving a short stare? How do we keep from being burned by the fire in one another's eyes?

Even if we make up our minds to look frankly *at* another person, should we look at their whole body or pick out one feature: a shoulder or an ear? Or should we concentrate on the face? Even then there are many ways of looking at a face. We can look slightly out of focus or just past the face or through it. We can choose to let our eyes rest on the surface of the skin or at varying degrees of depth. Again, should we look at the whole face or settle on the nose, the mouth, the eyes, or the mole on the cheek?

Let's say we narrow our gaze down to the eyes. Even then another wide range of choices comes into play. Do we look just in front of the eyes, at their surface, or candidly *into* them? Peering into a pair of eyes, once again we have a choice of focusing at varying degrees of depth. How deep will we go? If we look down and down into another's eyes, before long we are looking upon the heart. In polite society this is not done.

How polite should we be? How close do we really want to get to other people? The eyes are the window of the soul, but many of us live in windowless houses and never visit anyone else. "Eyes have they, but they see not," said Jesus. Scripture tells us to seek God's face. But we need to seek each other's faces, too.

Still another way of looking at others is to look not just with the eyes but with the whole face, lining up eyes, nose, mouth, and even ears with the other person's until we have a comfortable match. Sound goofy? Try it. Try this with someone close to you, someone safe, and then experiment with others. Singing instructors teach us to sing with all we've got, projecting sound through eyes and ears and out the top of our heads. It's the same with looking.

How much do you want to see? How much are you willing to reveal? The word *intimacy* can be broken down into the little phrase *in-to-me-see*. Isn't it true that we see only as much of others as we reveal of ourselves? Sadly, we tend to stick with acceptable social boundaries, letting each relationship settle at a point just short of intimacy.

What if we were to push the boundaries a little? What if we were to learn the habit of lovingly moving toward others? Isn't the kingdom of heaven a gentle invasion of personal space? If we are not taking deliberate steps to draw closer to others, chances are we are hurtling apart.

Instead of seeing people, we're good at keeping them just out of focus, looking past or through them, avoiding direct looks, never touching anyone with our eyes. How cold and alienating this is! Why do we do it? Because this way, we do not have to care. We can look at people all day long, but we see them only as we care for them. Love makes people visible.

My friend Carol Rose told me about the final days of caring for a dying friend. As the life of this dear woman slipped away, normal social boundaries relaxed. It became acceptable, even necessary, for Carol to look at her friend for long periods, savoring the last light in this loved one's face, which seemed to glow more brightly even as it faded. How hungry we all are just to see one another! Carol's looking was like the slaking of a deep thirst. It was like bathing in the river of life. And why not? Into that small room where two friends were together for the last time on earth, the kingdom of heaven was breaking. Laws were suspended, walls crumbled. The veil was parting, the mist in the eyes was clearing. The glory of God came down.

CHAPTER 32

Listening

Looking and listening are closely linked. Engaged in a conversation, I'll often find myself tuning out the other person's words and instead simply gazing at them, basking in their immediacy. I never understood this until I learned that only about 7 percent of communication is conveyed through words. The rest we read between the lines in the form of expressions, gestures, vocal inflection, the general energy people give off—in a word, their *presence*. To communicate well, it is more important to *watch* what people say, to *feel* what is being said, than to listen to every word. We must learn to hear with our eyes and heart.

We will never see other people if the air is dense with our own words. James had much to say about this: "Everyone should be quick to listen, slow to speak," and "If anyone considers himself religious and yet does not keep a tight rein on his tongue, he deceives himself and his religion is worthless" (1:19,26).

Good listening is a matter of becoming empty before people so as to sense when to speak, when not to, and how. There is a feeling that comes when our words are connecting with others. Most people keep on talking regardless of whether their words are hitting home. This is as senseless as yakking into a telephone without first placing the call. If I want to communicate with someone by phone, I must dial his number. Dialing my own number will not result in communication.

The goal of listening is to open a channel or connection along which communication may flow. The connection itself is more important than any words that are spoken. With a good connection, we can say anything we like. But if the connection is bad, our conversation may be ever so brilliant and yet mean nothing to the other person. Such talk is not only cheap, but offensive and intimidating. We'd be better to keep quiet.

"The first duty of love is to listen," observed Paul Tillich. A person who does not listen to others does not listen to God either. Indeed what we aim for with other people could be described as a form of prayer. Perhaps prayer is the wrong word, but what other word is there for spiritual communication? To communicate with God we drop all our masks, excuses, defenses, and in naked vulnerability we bare our hearts to Him. We set aside the flesh so as to commune heart to heart. Does it not work the same with people?

When we speak of a "heart-to-heart talk," don't we really mean becoming spiritual with one another? If this is not prayer, it looks and feels a lot like prayer. Whether there are many words or few, what is important is not the words but a mutual sense of openness, of attentive listening and receptivity. In this atmosphere what words there are take on a different quality from the words of ordinary conversation. They may be free flowing or halting, confident or searching, but they have the feel of words spoken in a cathedral or in a hushed forest clearing. There is the freedom for long silences that seem more articulate than words. This is spiritual communication, and it behaves like the wind, like one's own breathing.

One good rule of listening is that if you don't have anything to say, don't say anything. Many people are natural chatterboxes, and even quiet types often feel insecure about their quietness. Thus whether we talk or remain silent, the chattering still goes on in our heads. If we talk we say nothing; if we keep quiet, we hear nothing. While others are talking, we are busy formulating clever responses. The hardest job any of us have is to still the flapping tongue in our brains.

Attentive listening to a chatterbox is sometimes the one way to shut that person up. It is difficult to jabber away meaninglessly to someone who is truly listening. The act of listening invites a chatterer (if anything can) to listen to themselves. It's like standing in a crowd and staring up into the sky. Soon others are craning their necks too, wondering what is so interesting up there. Good listening points people to the wide-open sky of the great silence of God.

Listening to people teaches us to listen to God. Do you find God to be silent? It may be because He is listening to you chatter.

CHAPTER 33

Unknowing

To come to know other people, we must begin by admitting that we do not know them. By setting aside all assumptions, we open ourselves to mystery and so to love.

"'My thoughts are not your thoughts, neither are your ways my ways,' declares the LORD" (Isaiah 55:8). God is radically different from us—not just infinitely greater but categorically different. He is His own person, separate, distinct. Nothing could be truer than the statement that His thoughts are not our thoughts. In His presence we must unthink our thoughts. All prayer begins, not just with an acceptance of this fact, but with an enjoyment of it. The prospect of being with someone utterly different from ourselves becomes not threatening, but intriguing and delightful. By relaxing into this phenomenon, we are bound to learn something new, even astonishing. In the company of such a person, anything might happen!

What if we took this same approach in our relationships with people? Isn't it true that the thoughts of others are not our thoughts, their ways are not our ways? Naturally social conformity dulls the edge of these contrasts. People strive to be like each other, afraid that their differences will not be accepted. Yet underneath, the thoughts of all hearts are truly unique and distinct. Our thoughts are so much our own that they are entirely unknowable unless the owner chooses to reveal them. "Who among men knows the thoughts of a man except the man's spirit within him?" (1 Corinthians 2:11).

To say that we do not know each other, therefore, is quite true. This is a valid underlying premise in all relationships. Even a husband and wife of fifty years, if they are honest, will admit that in some deep, essential way, they still do not know one another. Indeed this mysterious unknowing is the mainspring of their love. Unknowing keeps love fresh and green.

Of course, it is also true that we can and do know other people. The people we are close to we know well. We know them so well, in fact, that there is no need to cling to our knowledge or insist on it. By insisting, we limit ourselves to what we already know, almost as if this knowledge might slip away if we do not hold on to it tightly. In some ways the human brain resembles a clenched fist; certainly it is often used that way. But the harder we clench, the more we limit ourselves. The fact is, we know what we know; we cannot suddenly unknow our knowledge. It is ours, hard won. It is simply there. Why cling so tightly?

This realization frees us to set aside our knowledge and act as if we do not know it. It is still there, ours for keeps, but by abrogating what we know already, we gain the advantage of acquiring new knowledge. We enter the sacred precincts of mystery. Each contact with another person now becomes an opportunity for surprise, for brand-newness, for rich delight, and for the gaining of wisdom. In each relationship we live experimentally, at the edge of discovery.

Not knowing becomes no threat but a playful freedom from the boredom of knowing.

To embrace unknowing is to descend from the mind into the heart. The result, whether in our prayer life or in our social life, is intimacy. The more we embrace unknowing, the better we shall know and be known. It is hard to become intimate with a know-it-all. Intimacy depends not on knowing but on vulnerability and trust. In a trusting relationship every encounter is an exploration and a discovery. Wrapped up in ourselves, we fear what we know. But together we can enter dark caves we would never think of entering alone.

"We know that we all possess knowledge. Knowledge puffs up, but love builds up" (1 Corinthians 8:1). How tempting it is to base our lives on knowledge—for we know so much! Unfortunately, with all knowledge the knowledge of evil is mixed with that of good, causing knowers to live with wariness, canniness, calculation. Only a deliberate policy of unknowing will untie this knot and restore to us the innocence of the Garden.

Satan tempted Eve to eat from the Tree of Knowledge by saying, "Your eyes will be opened, and you will be like God, knowing good and evil" (Genesis 3:5). This was a lie, because evil cannot really be known. Even God refuses to know evil, and hence He will say to evildoers, "I never knew you. Away from me!" (Matthew 7:23).

The idea that evil can be known and mastered is the supreme temptation. This is the original sin into which Satan fell and into which he is still trying to pull the world. To eat from the Tree of Knowledge is to become like Satan, not like God. To be like God is to resist the temptation to know evil along with good, and to eat instead only from the Tree of Life. We undo the damage done by eating from the Tree of Knowing by eating from the Tree of Unknowing.

I once saw this Tree of Unknowing. It was wintertime, and for many months I had been in a season of struggle and barrenness. One day while walking through the woods, I found myself gazing at a small, bare tree. There was nothing remarkable about this tree; it was just like any other. There was no reason to stand gawking, except that as I did so, the Lord spoke to me more clearly than I had heard Him for a long time. He said, "You see this leafless little tree? Soon it will be covered with foliage. In the same way your life, which now feels barren, will soon be bursting with abundance."

And lo, just as the Lord promised, it came to pass!

Have you found your Tree of Unknowing? To see it requires a spare and chastened gaze. When Moses saw this tree, it was on fire! My tree, I think, was just as wonderful, for it burned with a green flame, the fire of hope.

CHAPTER 34

Light One Candle

We waste a lot of time worrying about who people are not when we could be focusing on who they are. Isn't it strange how all of a person's good qualities can be obscured by the one point at which they cross us and refuse to change? Why not give up grappling with the bad and be thankful for the good?

When I recognize and focus on the goodness in others, I release that goodness to be a blessing to myself. If I never sincerely praise another's generosity or kindness, I will never personally benefit from those qualities. All I will see is the other's bad temper or stubbornness. "To the pure, all things are pure" (Titus 1:15). To see purity in another, I must be pure myself. I must look with the eyes of a pure heart.

In the same way, when I am irked by another's anger, it is because of my own bad temper. The other person's anger angers me; it is the same quality in us both. Therefore Jesus taught, "Do not judge, or you too will be judged" (Matthew 7:1). If focusing on the goodness in others blesses me, then focusing on their faults curses me.

In the beginning God made people good. All of us have sinned, choosing to be bad and so betray our created nature. But the capacity for goodness remains in each one and can always be revived. Will we aid and abet the fall by punishing others for their badness? Why not instead aid redemption by seeing and recovering people's goodness?

The Old Testament contains hundreds of astonishingly detailed prophecies concerning the life of Jesus. Do you not think that God has just as clear an idea of who each person is, how each life will unfold and glorify Him? Love sees and trusts in the God-authored plans for people. Just as there are millions of idols but only one true God, there are countless ways to idolize or falsify another person, but only one way to love that one. Love zeros in on the true person underneath all the sham and confusion.

Let people make wrong choices and indulge their false selves if they insist. But let us, meanwhile, stand beside the door of their true selves, inviting them to come home. Let us woo others home by pulling up their favorite chair before the hearth, nostalgically playing their favorite songs, and setting before them the food of their heart's desire.

However much darkness or trouble surrounds a life, always a light shines somewhere. If we were trapped with this person in a blizzard and had only one match, wouldn't we bend all our efforts toward nourishing this one small flame in hopes of getting a good fire going? Better to light one candle, says a Chinese proverb, than to curse the darkness.

Love means identifying exactly what people need that I can give, and giving it. I cannot give anyone else's gifts; I can only give of myself. There is a divine match between gift and need, between giver and recipient. There is also a divine time for each act of love, and that time is the present. I can get so caught up in the guilt of my lovelessness that I miss loving the one person I am with. Instead of worrying about all the people I do not love, I can ask, "Who *do* I love? Who can I love today?"

The Christian life is one of walking in the light, not stumbling around in the darkness. Where is the light of love shining for you right now? Start today with the one person you love. Take that one by the hand, look into those eyes, and say, "The thing I love best about you right now is..." Then maybe tomorrow you can love someone else. Don't take on the whole world all at once. Love people one by one. The will of God is what you *can* do, not what you cannot.

CHAPTER 35

Hate

There are some people who seem (at least to our eyes) to have little good in them. Or perhaps some maddening flaw tragically obscures their good. Such people may have a powerful presence in our lives, but not one we care to cultivate. Rather than practicing their presence, we practice their absence. We wish they would go away.

Another word for this is *hate*. Hatred is wishing people would get lost or (which amounts to the same thing) wishing we could bend them to our will. I remember distinctly the people I have hated and also how much I have grown through learning to love them.

Two examples spring to mind. One was the pastor of an early church I attended. Full of idealistic fervor, I came to this church expecting to turn it on its ear. After two years, however, I found myself up against a wall of unyielding traditionalism, and I fastened on the pastor as the chief culprit. At first I had felt successful in befriending him. But as time wore on he seemed threatened by the radicalness of my aims. I, in turn, realized that he was unwilling to change, and relations between us cooled.

One Sunday I arrived early at church and was surprised to see the pastor playing hymns on a guitar. Normally the preservice music was provided by a tiny gray-haired woman at a baby grand piano. But she was absent today, and the pastor was fulfilling her duties in addition to his own. Until then I hadn't even known he played the guitar. He wasn't great at it, but I was touched. Listening to his plaintive strums, I began to reflect on all the various jobs this man did to serve his small flock—teaching classes, visiting the sick, chairing meetings, marrying and burying and baptizing, sharing the lessons of his life week by week in homespun sermons, and now offering us his music. What was so wrong about all of this? On the contrary, suddenly his life seemed to me to be full of good.

In this frame of mind, the differences of opinion I had with him began to fall away, and I saw him in a new light. I saw him, seated there in the sanctuary, as if bathed in a warm and radiant glow. It was just as if a light from heaven were shining upon him. As my heart softened and opened, I began to comprehend secrets. I felt the force of the opposition against this man, the personal obstacles he faced, the struggles and sorrows of a lifetime. And I saw too how, against incredible odds, he was being faithful to his Lord and living a good life. For a few moments I felt the purity and simplicity of the light of God shining through this homely clay vessel, and it left me full of wonder, tenderness, and gratitude.

I would like to say that I remained in this state of illumination and learned to love this man. But I did not. In those days I did not know the voice of the Lord; I did not even realize (until years later) that God had spoken to me that morning. And so my heart quickly closed again. Instead of accepting the forgiveness and love that the

Lord was offering me, I descended deeper into hate and eventually left that church in angry woundedness.

A second example dates from a later period in my life. I formed a business partnership with an unusually gifted man, but almost from the beginning we ran into trouble. As much as I valued his admirable qualities, I never quite felt comfortable with him. I understand now that strong people have strong failings and that they require strong and gentle love. But at the time, unable to give such love, my response instead was a growing frustration that waxed into hatred.

After a stormy five-year relationship, our business venture drew to a close, and my partner decided (to my great relief) to move to another part of the country. His friends threw a farewell party for him, and naturally I was there, though with some mixed feelings. As we were all Christians, toward the end of the evening we gathered around our friend to pray for him and bless him. I was not keen on this, but I knew it was important. Though I had made some progress in resolving my chaotic feelings toward him, I knew something more was necessary.

I would never have dreamed that the something more would come so easily as I rested my hand on his shoulder that night and silently blessed him. We prayed for about twenty minutes. While others prayed aloud, I remained quiet and found myself reflecting (much as in the previous case) on the essential worth of this man as a human being. I saw the mountainous struggles he faced and their source in his childhood. Gradually I realized that every bad quality I had seen in him was present also in me. I too was a controller. I too shrank from intimacy. All along, my relationship with him had been based on my own selfish ambition. I had wanted and expected the moon from him, but I had never been humble enough to enter into his presence to see him as he is.

All this and much more came clear to me during that short time of resting my human hand on a very human shoulder. In the quietness I realized that in all the years I had known this man, I had never practiced his presence. As much as I thought I had learned to listen to God, I had never bothered to listen to the heart of this child of His.

On this occasion, I did not forget what God showed me as the door of secrets opened. In those twenty minutes I began to love a man I had hated. After this I would never be the same.

CHAPTER 36

Jacob

*A*ny man who is deeply alienated from his twin brother is going to be alienated from everyone else, too, but most of all from himself.

This is the story of Jacob, whose whole life was twisted by one person he hated: his brother, Esau. Although these two were twins, they had radically different personalities and lived separate lives. Jacob was a mama's boy, while the manly Esau was his father's favorite. We can imagine the family dynamics!

At his mother's goading, Jacob impersonated his brother and so tricked their elderly father, Isaac, into giving him the blessing that was rightfully Esau's. In this way, Jacob learned early on that if he was ever going to get ahead in life, he had to do it by pretending to be someone he was not. In himself he was not good enough. Even his mother, the person who loved him most, could not trust him to succeed except by pretense. The name *Jacob* means "deceiver." The result of deceiving others is to live in fear of them. So Jacob was forced to flee in fear from Esau, who was angry enough to kill him.

Since pretenders attract other pretenders, the next milestone in

Jacob's life was to be tricked into marrying Leah, a woman he did not love. Even Rachel, the woman he did love, was an idol worshiper who for many years was unable to bear children. And so it went, one problem after another. Jacob could never win. Though he prospered materially, it was only by trickery. While outwardly he grew more and more successful, inwardly he was a man who lived in fear.

Eventually the time came for him to return home and face Esau. On the way there, strange to say, God met him in the form of a man who engaged him in a wrestling match. Already the Lord had revealed Himself to Jacob spiritually, but this had never been enough to win him over. It wasn't until God got physical with Jacob that Jacob got serious with God. Isn't the same true of us? We can have a good spiritual notion of God, but until we experience Him physically through the man Jesus Christ, we do not really know Him.

When God got physical, Jacob cried out, "I will not let you go unless you bless me." Jacob longed, as we all do, to be blessed. More than just to *be* blessed, he longed to *feel* blessed. Already he had extracted a blessing from his father, but that one didn't feel good. Now he wanted a real blessing. He wanted a blessing he could feel right down to his toes. He wanted to be blessed simply for who he was.

God came through for Jacob that day, but in a way that Jacob didn't quite get. All he got from wrestling with God was a wrenched hip that left him limping and still terrified of meeting Esau. Jacob was so afraid that he arranged to send Esau extravagant gifts in an effort to pacify him: hundreds of goats, sheep, camels, donkeys, and cattle. All these droves he sent on ahead, carefully instructing his servants to present them to Esau with lavish condescension. After so many years, Jacob still thought to pull the wool over his brother's eyes.

In the same way, don't we too break our necks trying to appear successful, happy, loving and kind in the eyes of others, when really we are terrified that no one will ever accept us as we are?

Jacob, however, was in for a big surprise. The thing he most feared—the meeting with Esau—would turn out to be the greatest blessing of his life. Scripture's account of this meeting is one of the most beautiful and poignant moments in literature: Jacob "bowed down to the ground seven times as he approached his brother. But Esau ran to meet Jacob and embraced him; he threw his arms around his neck and kissed him. And they wept" (Genesis 33:3-4).

Did Jesus, in describing the prodigal son's reunion with his father, intentionally echo this scene? Surely nothing so embodies the love of God as reconciliation between family members. What an overwhelming relief for Jacob to be accepted in the very place he had felt the most wounded and rejected! He himself tells Esau, "To see your face is like seeing the face of God, now that you have received me favorably" (Genesis 33:10).

The previous night, Jacob had met God physically, seen Him face to face, and touched Him. But where he really met God, and where he finally received the fullness of blessing for which he so ached, was in the arms of his brother. Wrestling with God, Jacob was wounded, but in meeting Esau he was healed. No experience of his life was greater or deeper, more spiritual or more wonderful, than seeing the glory of God in a human face.

CHAPTER 37

The Crossroads

*T*he fact that we can gain so much from people we have hated is nowhere more true than in our relationship with Jesus Christ. Part of the power of the cross is that it brings us to the point of our hatred of God. The cross is all that we do not want God to be, all that we resent Him for, all the bitter heaviness of our lives, all the pain that so oppresses us that we must find a scapegoat, must pin the blame on someone else. And who better to blame than Jesus?

Before we can love God freely and unconditionally, we must come to the cross of Christ and have all this poison exposed and drawn out. In the same way, before we can love people we must encounter the point of our hatred. Each person we meet will bring us in a unique way to the crossroads of love and hate.

None of us likes to admit that there are people we hate. But why not call a spade a spade? Relationships are awkward and messy, and hatred is the frustration we feel at not being able to control them. We'd like to nail people down so that we wouldn't have to deal with the complexity of always trying to hit a moving target. The crucifixion of Christ is the ultimate symbol of this nailing down. We tried to pin God, to get Him to hold still long enough that we could cram Him into a box. Thank goodness He escaped our grasp to prove forever that love is stronger than hate.

Hate is not so much the opposite of love as its absence. If we are not busy loving, we are busy hating. At the cross this fact loses its subtlety and becomes crystal clear. The cross is high noon at the equator of life. There are no shadows here, no gray areas. There is only love and hate, light and darkness. Hence John writes, "Anyone who claims to be in the light but hates his brother is still in the darkness. Whoever loves his brother lives in the light, and there is nothing in him to make him stumble" (1 John 2:9-10).

If we find ourselves stumbling, it is because of hate. We tend not to recognize hate because it is so common, so garden-variety. When the serpent came to Eve in the garden, his appearance was probably not glorious but quite ordinary. What caught Eve's attention was not his appearance, but his voice. How strange that this lowly serpent, unlike any of the other animals, could talk! No wonder James called the tongue "a world of evil" that "corrupts the whole person, sets the whole course of his life on fire, and is itself set on fire by hell" (3:6).

The way we use our tongue reveals the hate or the love in our hearts. Even more revealing than what we say aloud is our interior noise, that wormy little tongue that keeps waggling in our minds. It's fine to say that temptation is not sin and that we needn't give in to this noise. But all too often, this whispering alien voice does rule us. If we loved more, our garden would be more peaceful, and we would pay less heed to the serpent's voice and hear more readily the still small voice of the Lord.

Hate has many faces, many forms. When we can no longer tolerate the ugliness of one form of hatred, we move on to the next. From fear we move to condemnation, from condemnation to repression, from repression to grudging acceptance, from grudging acceptance to pleasant civility, and on and on. We are like insomniacs tossing restlessly from side to side, trying to get comfortable on a bed of nails. Always there is war within us. Sometimes the war is hot and sometimes it is cold, but seldom is there pure and simple peace.

My friend Ron Reed wrote a play entitled *Remnant*. One character in the play, named Loner, was a wild, dark, criminal type, almost an animal. He wore leather and studs and also an ugly metal appendage attached to one of his arms like a mechanical claw. If anyone came near Loner, he brandished this claw like a weapon that was a part of himself. Here was a man in the grip of hatred, a man at war with himself.

In the climactic scene of this play, Loner experienced a breakthrough that compelled him to perform a strange action. Approaching a Christmas tree in the center of the stage, Loner removed his huge metal claw and hung it there like a grisly ornament.

What a powerful moment this was! Many years later, I still often ponder it, especially as it pertains to my own program of personal disarmament, my own efforts to root out hate in my life and to divest myself of every self-defense against love. Many times I have pictured myself literally taking off some ugly mask or artificial appendage and placing it at the foot of the cross. The Christmas tree we decorate with beautiful ornaments, but the cross of Christ we decorate with our ugliest deformities.

CHAPTER 38

Confrontation

Lovelessness often results from an inability to confront others in a healthy way. There is a time and a place and a manner for confrontation, but most of us shy away from this important work and so end up simmering in quiet rage. Perhaps with some people we have tried many times to speak our minds, yet each attempt has only produced further alienation. How often have our well-intentioned efforts backfired as those we seek to reach grow defensive and angry or else retreat further into their shells? Then we in turn grow less and less willing to intervene and more and more skeptical of seeing positive results.

There can be no answer to this dilemma until we learn to honor other people enough to enter their presence. We enter the presence of people in the same way that we enter the presence of God: by submission. This means abandoning all judgments, all agendas, all preconceptions, and seeing and accepting people as they are. How can we presume to confront what people are not if we will not first confront who they are?

When Jesus confronted a woman caught in adultery, He first defended her by confronting her enemies. Having disarmed and driven off all those who would judge her, Jesus said, "Neither do I condemn you." Only then, as the sinner stood there free from all condemnation, did Jesus exhort her, "Go now and leave your life of sin" (John 8:11). In this way Jesus taught that no one can say to another human being, "Go and sin no more," without first saying and demonstrating wholeheartedly, "I do not condemn you."

We think we know so well what other people need. Often enough we do. But before we can tell what we know, we must first, paradoxically, forget we ever knew it. We must enter the fire of a person's living presence and accept the risk of spontaneous, unpremeditated relationship. Only in the midst of the free fall of real personal encounter may we discover, when we least expect it, the wisdom to confront a thorny problem.

Whenever possible, it is best to let others take the lead in correcting themselves. It is surprising how willing many are to do this if only they catch a whiff of genuine love. In this atmosphere, as often as not, the forbidden issue will actually be raised by the other person first, and suddenly we're invited to give the counsel stored up within us. Alternatively, once we come to know and appreciate others, it may no longer seem so important to give them a piece of our mind!

A good confrontation leaves no mess to clean up. Since we do not condemn, no condemnation sticks to us. We have everything to gain, but nothing to lose. If the other listens to us, good. If not, it is not our problem. Paul warned, "If someone is caught in a sin, you who are spiritual should restore him gently. But watch yourself, or you also may be tempted" (Galatians 6:1). Note that confrontation is to be done by those who are "spiritual." Woe unto us if, in the course of correcting others, we ourselves stoop to carnal methods!

As the people of Israel crossed the Jordan River into the Promised Land, they were commanded to follow the ark of the covenant, which was the presence of God. "Then you will know which way to go," instructed Joshua, "since you have never been this way before" (Joshua 3:4). When it comes to people, we travel in uncertain territory. We are seldom sure how to proceed. It goes without saying that we can do nothing without the presence of God, but we must also wait upon the presence of people. If in this waiting we give others an opportunity to sense our humble respect, they may feel safe enough to emerge from hiding and present themselves to us.

After crossing the Jordan, shortly before the battle of Jericho, Joshua met a man with a drawn sword and asked him, "Are you for us or for our enemies?" The surprising answer was, "Neither.... But as commander of the army of the LORD I have now come." The man Joshua met was the pre-incarnate Christ, and He had but one message for Joshua: "Take off your sandals, for the place where you are standing is holy" (Joshua 5:13-15).

As we contemplate confrontation with another person, it is good to remember that Jesus is on neither side. Fighting for peace and love is not like fighting for anything else. Confrontation is holy ground, and we would be well advised to take off our shoes—especially if those shoes are steel-toed and spiked! Removing one's shoes is a gesture of humble submission, of surrender. All spiritual warfare begins with surrender. Entering the promised land of loving relationships will not happen without a fight, but the real fight is with our own willfulness. The battle is the Lord's, not ours. The way to fight is through surrender and loving service, first of all to Him and then to one another.

CHAPTER 39

Sweet Surrender

Once a woodcutter, weary after a day's work, was trudging home through the forest. Along the narrow road came a stranger in a carriage who stopped to offer him a ride. Gratefully, the woodcutter climbed into the carriage, and the two men fell into conversation as they proceeded through the forest.

After a while the carriage emerged into a broad clearing that, to the surprise of the woodcutter, was filled with a great throng of people.

Immediately he asked his host, "What are all these people doing here?"

"They're waiting for the king," responded the carriage driver.

"And how will we know when the king arrives?" asked the woodcutter.

"When the king arrives," answered the driver, "all these people will take off their hats."

At that precise moment, a deep hush fell over the clearing, and all the people in the crowd reverently removed their hats. Glancing at his companion, the woodcutter saw that the driver of the carriage was still wearing his hat.

"Out of all these people," said the woodcutter, "you and I are the only ones who have not removed our hats."

"You are right," said his friend. "That must mean that one of us is the king."

Whereupon the woodcutter, in a moment of profound recognition, humbly doffed his hat.

This is a story of recognition and surrender. We surrender to Christ when we recognize Him as our rightful King. But does our submission end here? Will we bow before our King only to lord it over His subjects? Scripture teaches, "Clothe yourselves with humility toward one another" (1 Peter 5:5). There is really no one to whom we should not doff our hat. There is no one so low, so difficult, so mean, or so bad as to be unworthy of our profound respect.

Love is surrender. Did not Jesus surrender to the whole world when He died on the cross? In doing so He showed us the way we are to follow. He showed us that we are to submit to other people not because they are good or perfect but precisely because they are not perfect, and so stand in need of our love.

"Submit to one another out of reverence for Christ" (Ephesians 5:21). We do not worship people, but when we worship Jesus, the God-man, we learn something about how to enter into the presence of all people and stand amazed. We learn to be meek and humble, poor in spirit and pure in heart, and to throw away all our bristling weaponry of fear, mistrust, jealousy, and aggression. We learn to put on our best behavior not only for God but for everyone. We learn that the way we behave when we know God is watching is the same way we should behave in the presence of people.

One day Jeremiah was looking at the flowering branch of an almond tree when he became aware that God was watching him. In that moment Jeremiah realized that God was always watching "to see that my word is fulfilled" (1:12). If God has eyes in almond trees and in every blade of grass, then how much more is He watching us through the eyes of our fellow humans!

Communion

The Christian life begins with an act of surrender to God through Jesus Christ. And it continues in the same way. Each step forward is essentially the same as the first: a step of surrender. And the result of each surrender is the same, for the Lord always responds to the giving up of our life with the giving of His. Far from being diminished by this process, we are made inestimably richer by being filled with the Holy Spirit. Through humbling our minds and our wills, we make way for God's mind and will to flow into us.

This same mystery lies at the heart of human relationships. Submitting to others in love, we make way for their spirits to commingle with ours. In a sense we are indwelled by the spirits of those we love, in a way that does not threaten our own identity but rather makes us more ourselves. No longer is it necessary to try to figure out or compete with others, for we begin to understand people from the inside out. We see why they have certain foibles and fears, why they are the way they are. The inherent differences between personalities, rather than worrying or frightening us, become a source of quiet wonder.

No longer striving to be complete in ourselves, we allow others to complete us.

Welcome to the body of Christ! Without this mystical communion with other souls, we feel cut off not only from people but from God. For people are the primary channel through which God gives Himself to us. In fact the essential way we are to submit to God is by submitting to one another. A certain religiosity may cause us to humble ourselves before God. But unless we also humble ourselves before people, we are fooling ourselves. Relationships with people are the litmus test of our holiness.

We are meant to live in close communion with others. God wants us to be brought to complete unity through the intermingling of our spirits. The only way this can happen is through mutual submission. One spirit must stand aside to let another spirit come in. We do this easily enough when a guest comes to our home. Outwardly we make every effort to be the perfect host. But what if we opened our heart to others as well as our home? When Jesus visited the home of Martha and Mary, He rebuked Martha not only for shutting Him out with her busy-ness, but for shutting out her sister as well. Do we, too, play host to Jesus while snubbing other people?

"Where two or three come together in my name," said Jesus, "there am I with them" (Matthew 18:20). To "come together" could refer to a prayer meeting, but it might just as easily be a visit over coffee or a chance meeting with strangers at the bus stop. Jesus' point is not that we end every prayer with the words "in Christ's name," but that in all our circumstances we remain soft and open toward others.

When two people open their hearts to one another, one new

heart forms between them. When I became a Christian, I asked Jesus
to come into my heart, and He did. If I want to know true fellowship with others, the first step is the same: to make a decision to join
my heart with theirs. Then together we ask Jesus to come into the
one new heart that has been formed between us. And He does! He
does because He promised He would.

We'll know when the door of our heart opens, for something in
us relaxes and our relationships become characterized by spontaneity,
freshness, laughter, caring, and a natural intimacy. We begin to shine
not only with our own radiance, but with the glory of others. Indeed
we are meant to become lamps in which the light of others shines
and so is magnified. We are designed to be givers of glory, first to
God and then to everyone else. We cannot have glory without giving
it, nor can we give glory to others without being glorified ourselves.

Is our goal to match wits with others or to mix spirits? In the
house of communion everyone shines.

CHAPTER 41

Cathedral

Entering the presence of another human being is like entering a cathedral. The appropriate response is awe. With our eyes open to the wonder of another person, suddenly we are in the presence of something greater than ourselves. Even though we too are human, somehow the other is greater than we are, because the other draws us out of ourselves. We find that we are made with a capacity for awe that only another person can fill.

In Raymond Carver's short story "Cathedral," the protagonist is a sullen, thickheaded military man whose wife is starved for his love. One evening this couple is visited by a blind man, a friend of the wife's from years before who has kept up a correspondence with her. Although there is no hint of an affair, the blind man has obviously cultivated a depth of intimacy with the wife that makes his visit intensely threatening to the husband.

Following a politely awkward dinner and some strained conversation, the television is turned on. Eventually the wife falls asleep, leaving her husband and the blind man alone together on the couch. The two stay up late smoking and drinking in the eerie glare of the

TV, and in the wee hours of the morning a program comes on about cathedrals. Something captivates the husband's attention, and before long he finds himself trying to describe a cathedral to a man who, blind from birth, has never seen one. Words fail him, and one thing leads to another, until in the final scene the two men are on their hands and knees on the living room floor, with the husband drawing a picture of a cathedral while the blind man holds his drawing hand to get a feel for the thing.

It is a strange and startling moment of raw, visceral intimacy. The husband, surprised into vulnerability, tells us that this experience "was like nothing else in my life up to now." Kneeling there on the floor beside the blind man who moments before had been not only a stranger, but a feared enemy, the shaken husband whispers in awe, "This is really something."[3]

What has happened? A man who until now has lived entirely inside the hell of his own skull suddenly has an experience that moves him beyond himself. He actually says, "I was in my own house. I knew that. But I didn't feel like I was inside anything." What cracks him open? Nothing more than a moment of intimacy with a fellow human being.

A cathedral is one of the few buildings large enough to give us, even while we are inside it, a sense of being outside. This is why cathedrals are built, to create this peculiar impression and so give us a taste of the transcendence of God.

But a cathedral is nothing compared to a person. After all, "the Most High does not live in houses made by men" (Acts 7:48). No, He lives in the people themselves. "Don't you know that you yourselves are God's temple?" (1 Corinthians 3:16). Because human beings bear God's image, they mediate His presence. With our physical eyes we are not going to see God in this life. But we do see people.

When the husband in Carver's story gets down on the floor with the blind man to draw pictures like a kindergarten kid, he has a redefining experience. Everything he thought he knew—about blindness, about himself, about people and life in general—suddenly crumbles before the dawning of a great new light. This is how problems are solved: through a redefining experience. According to Albert Einstein, "The significant problems we face cannot be solved by the same level of thinking that created them." In a sense this is what people are for: to break our molds and lift us to new levels of thinking. If we never humble ourselves enough to be broken by our relationships, we cannot discover the fresh depths of awe and ecstasy that are available only in communion with others.

We are made for the awe and ecstasy of communion. We are made to be always seeking and discovering something greater than ourselves. This central need is expressed in the second of the twelve steps of Alcoholics Anonymous, which states, "We came to believe that a power greater than ourselves could restore us to sanity." The founders of AA knew that the problem of alcoholism (like all problems) can only be overcome by a spiritual experience. They knew too that the primary meaning of *spiritual* is *relational*. Nothing sickens or weakens us so much as isolation, as being trapped inside ourselves. To be whole and healthy we must have a redefining relational experience not just once in our lives, but every day.

In our burned-out, peopled-out, savagely codependent society, it is vital for the socially addicted to draw apart and encounter the living God in solitude, in personal devotion, in nature, or in cathedrals. Nothing can replace a one-on-one meeting with God. Still, there is more to religion than this. Our lives are fulfilled only when we start meeting God socially, in the midst of people. Only then will we experience our faith as not just a subjective phenomenon, but something objective and tangible, real and present. Then we know our God is with us. He is someone we can talk to, eat with, see with our own eyes, touch with our hands.

Then we too will say: *This is really something.*

PRACTICE

*Since it is necessary to devote much time and effort to acquiring this habit
you must not be discouraged when you fail since the habit is formed
only with difficulty;
but once you have acquired it, you will experience great joy.*
BROTHER LAWRENCE

*I*f the word *people* asks the question "Who?" and if *presence* raises the question "What?" then the word *practice* asks "How?" How exactly are we to practice the presence of people?

When Brother Lawrence used the phrase "the practice of the presence of God," he meant something specific that he explained over and over in clear, precise language. In brief, having decided "to give all to gain all," he developed a habit of "adoring God as often as I could, keeping my mind in His holy presence and recalling it as often as it wandered. I had no little difficulty in this exercise, but I kept on despite all difficulties and was not worried or distressed when I was involuntarily distracted." He testifies that "the effect of repeating these acts is that they become more habitual and the presence of God becomes, as it were, more natural."[1] Essentially his method consists of "an interior gaze on God which should always be quiet, humble and loving."[2]

When I speak of the practice of the presence of people, I too mean something that, though mysterious, is specific enough to be described and carried out. I mean emptying myself and contemplating people in much the same way that Brother Lawrence contemplated God. So specific is this practice that I know when I'm engaged in it and when I am not. As Brother Lawrence described "an interior gaze on God," I turn my inner eyes upon people. Abandoning the noise inside my own head, I let the person before me fill my thoughts and my field of vision. I say to my ego, "Excuse me, sir, but you'll have to stand aside right now. There's a human being who needs my full attention." If I miss my ego I can always pick him up again later on; there's no danger of losing my connection with him. But there's a great danger of not connecting with people. So I let the people I am with be larger and more mysterious than myself. I let them be wonderful. I make a point of enjoying each one, knowing that only by enjoying others will I enjoy myself.

The word *enjoy* is like the word *encourage*. Just as *encourage* means to put courage into someone else, so *enjoy* indicates a transfusion of joy. When I sincerely enjoy people, they feel this, and they leave my presence more joyful. When this happens, I too am happier, and I know that I am practicing the presence of people. The evidence is this transfusion of joy. All my relationships take on a rich glow of fulfillment. Even when a relationship is troubled, I can be satisfied that I have done everything in my power to let the other person shine. If I turn on a light switch and nothing happens, then I change the bulb. In relationships I keep changing the bulb until a connection is made.

This can be hard work. In some cases it feels like weeding an overgrown garden. But I make it my goal to see the beautiful flower, the handiwork of God, in every person. Rather than cultivating my own ideas about people, I cultivate their real presence. I open wide the eyes of my heart to see people (as nearly as possible) as they are, rather than through the screen of my personal prejudices.

But is all this even possible? Of course it is! Nothing but selfish idleness keeps us from it. While I do not claim to do this work perfectly, I do give myself to it more and more with increasingly satisfying results. Jesus Christ, in taking the form of a man, "made himself nothing" (Philippians 2:7), and we are bidden to do the same (see v.

5). Are you content to be nothing? Or are you still trying to put yourself forward and be somebody? The somebody you are striving to be will keep you from knowing anyone else. Let your goal be not to glorify yourself but to glorify others. Stand aside and let them shine—and then see how your own light blazes forth!

CHAPTER 42

An Experiment

*P*erhaps there is no one way to practice the presence of people. After all, letting you be you is not something I've ever done before with anyone else. Maybe there are as many ways to love as there are individuals and situations. But here's an experiment to try.

Give yourself to the next person you meet. Relax and become entirely present to the other. Whoever it is, act as if you have never seen this person before. Act as if you have never before seen another human being, period. Fool yourself into believing this. Tell yourself, "The face of the person I am looking at right now is stranger than the surface of the planet Pluto."

This odd statement is, after all, true. The surface of Pluto, the smallest and most remote planet in the solar system, has never been photographed, never been observed by human eyes. Similarly, no one has ever seen the face of the person before you as you are seeing it right now. For one thing, this moment is unique; it holds possibilities never before present. For another thing, no one else has ever looked through your eyes. Only you can do that. And the way you look changes things. The way you look at people changes the way they look.

It may be that no one else has ever bothered to look at the person before you in a way that changes anything. You could be the first. You might be the first one to pay this person the attention he or she deserves. You might be the first to see her possibilities and not her limitations. You might be the first to offer a look that says, "I give you permission to be completely yourself. This is all I want from you. Right now you are free to think, say, or do anything you like. I will not judge, confine, predict, or control you. I am not afraid of you or of your judgments of me."

You may try this approach and find that it does nothing for you. If so, then try something different. See if you can see the little child in grown people. Try this especially with those you have trouble getting along with. See the little girl or the little boy inside these oversized adult bodies. This child was there long before the adult armor was locked into place, before guile and scorn became second nature, before the weight of disillusionment descended like a hood to darken the whole complexion.

You see this large, puffy adult face before you? Let your mind drift back through the years until this face grows small again, pixieish, soft, bright, and glowing. Get back to this person's antediluvian world, before the great flood that swamped all their best feelings and dreams and left them wounded so deeply they have never recovered. See the spunk, the heroism, the natural joy, the pure, wild life that once lived in this person's little child and that is still there if only someone would come and call it forth like Lazarus from the tomb.

What we are after is to see living souls, to retrieve the image of God in fallen creatures. If you look at people in this way, they will know it. They will feel it. You will feel it too. You will like it. It will feel different. It will be better than anything you have ever tried before.

It will also be difficult. It will not be difficult while you are doing it, but it will be difficult to keep doing it. It will be difficult, at first, to believe that this practice is worthwhile, that anything will come of it. It will be difficult to begin this new way of looking, and it will be even more difficult to continue in it. Old habits die hard; new ones are not easily formed. Constantly your eyes will slip back into their lazy, restless, unloving blindness. Again and again you will have to remind yourself to return to a simple, open, trusting gaze. You will have to practice this. You will have to practice the presence of people.

This is exactly what Brother Lawrence said of the practice of the presence of God. He worked at it for years before reaping his amazing harvest of continual joy. Hence he urged, "Do not be discouraged by the resistance you will encounter."[3] Many times he reflected that "in the beginning a persistent effort is needed to form the habit of continually talking with God and to refer all we do to Him, but after a little care His love brings us to it without any difficulty."[4]

These last words are the key: "His love brings us to it." God rewards and aids by His grace every act of deliberately seeking His love. On our own we cannot do anything, nor are we expected to. We may feel as if we are acting alone, but all along God's love draws us. We can depend on this. He wants us to succeed. With only a little effort exerted in this direction, miracles will start happening. Moreover, if we persevere in discipline, a point finally comes when the balance tips in our favor. After this, everything that formerly seemed so hard begins to come "without any difficulty."

Here is Brother Lawrence's description of this event: "Just as I thought I must live out my life beset by difficulties and anxieties…I suddenly found myself changed and my soul, which up till then was always disturbed, experienced a profound interior peace as if it had found its center and a place of rest. Ever since then I have walked before God in simplicity and faith, with humility and love."[5]

In the same way, if you will commit yourself to the practice of the presence of people, you'll get good at it. Effort is always necessary to achieve anything worthwhile. But at a certain point in any spiritual discipline, the balance tips from effort to effortlessness. The new habit has taken shape. And one day, lo and behold, you wake up to discover that you really do love others as you love yourself, with a deep pure love that bubbles up irrepressibly like living water in your soul.

CHAPTER 43

Back to Basics

*T*he word *practice* can convey the notion that what is required is to work hard at being superaware of people, to concentrate with all our might, prop our eyelids open with toothpicks, and slap ourselves on the knuckles whenever our attention wanders.

But this is not the way of it. For the organ we use to practice people's presence is not our brain, nor our eyes, nor even our will power, but our heart.

The heart is a curious organ that, like a child, responds much better to suggestion than to command. Sternly tell the heart what it must do, and it will turn a cold shoulder to you. However, provide the heart with the right atmosphere, romance it with candles and violins, whisper tenderly in its ear, then do something unexpected while looking discreetly the other way, and all at once the heart will open like a flower.

Isn't this how God wooed the world? For centuries He issued commands and performed mighty wonders, all of which fell short of achieving our salvation. Then Jesus came, healing people, loving them, telling stories, saying and doing the most surprising things, and ultimately getting into trouble and hanging on a cross and dying. And that's what did it; that's what opened the human heart.

Through Jesus Christ, God got people's attention so that finally they noticed Him and learned to practice His presence in the world. To accomplish this end, it took not just the life of Jesus, but His death. It took the blood of Jesus. Because the heart is an organ of blood, it took the spilling of holy blood to cure humanity's hard-heartedness.

What the human heart desires most is to be clean and pure, and this state can only be achieved through washing with the blood of Christ. A guilty, impure heart is swamped in self-centered preoccupation. But a clean heart delights in loving God and people. Where does love come from? Paul tells us it "comes from a pure heart and a good conscience and a sincere faith" (1 Timothy 1:5). All the meditation and concentrated effort in the world cannot produce this result. Only sincere faith in the power of Jesus' blood can set the heart and the conscience free to love.

If our goal is to bring closer the stars of heaven, the tool we need is a powerful telescope. But even the finest telescope will give disappointing results if its lens is scratched and dirty. A highly sensitive instrument requires proper and delicate treatment. Just so, when it comes to the heart, we must cleanse and polish its lens with the one substance that is especially designed for that purpose—"the precious blood of Christ, a lamb without blemish or defect" (1 Peter 1:19).

Receiving and applying the blood of Christ is the way to open the heart and to practice the presence of people with sincere, deep love. If we find our consciences to be cloudy and troubled, and if our lives are not rich in love, we must consider the possibility that, however orthodox our theology may be, we have somehow missed the point of Christianity and we must go back to square one.

We should never be ashamed to return to the drawing board. In fact all of us should return there every day like children playing on a chalkboard. The virtue of a chalkboard is that everything drawn on it can be wiped out and begun all over again. If we were children living in a cottage beside the sea, then every day we would rush out to the beach to play at drawing and building in the sand, and then every night the tide would wash our sandbox clean. As adults, we might perhaps consider this a pointless activity. But why cling so tightly to our grown-up accomplishments? What better way to live than with a clean slate every morning?

Consider the example of Brother Lawrence, who "asked to remain a novice always, not believing anyone would want to profess him, and unable to believe that his two years of novitiate had passed."[6] Even the truth, after all, is not something to be held on to doggedly. If something is really true, then let's learn it anew every day. And if there's anything we've acquired that is not true, that does not stand the test of heartfelt love, then let's wipe it away with the blood of Jesus!

This openhanded, teachable attitude is what is implied in the word *practice*. Inherent in this word is the freedom to experiment, to try and try again with limitless humility to fail. Practice makes perfect, but the practice itself is not perfect. Practice is a patient, relaxed process of finding out what works and what doesn't. Practice leaves plenty of room for making mistakes; indeed mistakes are taken for granted. In practice it goes without saying that any success is only the fruit of many failures. Hence the failure is as important as the success, for the one could not happen without the other.

Many people avoid practice because of the fear of failure. Perfectionists have the mistaken idea that something is not worth doing if they cannot look good by getting it right the first time. For the perfectionist, any misstep is an unpleasant and embarrassing surprise. But for a humble person, the surprise is getting it right. Humility expects trial and error and so rejoices all the more at success. Humility is always being surprised by grace.

Either life is practice, or it is performance. It cannot be both. Do you love surprises, or do you prefer to stay in control? Are you a professional at life or an amateur? Do you live spontaneously and experimentally for the sheer love of it? Or are you an expert who takes pride in being right about everything? Would you rather be right than happy?

None of us can be perfect. But everyone can be free. Which will you choose?

Chapter 44

Let God Be God

*I*f you want to be free, begin by having a God who is free. Let Him be free to do whatever He wants. He's going to anyway, whether you agree to it or not, so you might as well give Him your blessing. If He wants to work in your life through hardship, unemployment, sickness, marriage difficulties, or any other form of suffering, let Him do it. You're going to suffer anyway; it's guaranteed. So you might as well suffer well, in the way that is ordained for you at the present time. Set God free to be God in the midst of your suffering. He is greater than any trouble. He is greater precisely because He is beyond it all, totally free.

If you do not have a God who is free to do anything He pleases with your life, then you will not have a God who can set you free regardless of your circumstances. Instead you will have a conditional God, one who will be real to you only when your children are well behaved, your debts paid, your diseases healed. You will have a king who is king only in heaven and not on earth. God preserve us from such a narrow, wicked little substitute for Him!

Does God want to strip you of your job, your money, your reputation?

Let Him!

Does He want to sit up there in the sky having all the answers while you struggle away below in helpless bewilderment?

Let Him!

What if God wants to take one of your children to heaven?

Let Him!

What if He wants to condemn 90 percent of the world's people to everlasting hell?

Let Him!

Don't just let Him do all this, but praise Him for it. And don't just praise Him—love Him! Love Him unconditionally. If you want to know God's unconditional love, try loving Him that way.

Listen: "Woe to him who quarrels with his Maker, to him who is but a potsherd among the potsherds on the ground. Does the clay say to the potter, 'What are you making?' Does your work say, 'He has no hands'?" (Isaiah 45:9).

How much freedom do you want? Do you want to be completely free of shame and guilt and know that you are respected, cherished, and loved without limit? Do you want to be free to be fully, outrageously yourself? Do you want to be exactly who you are, no strings attached? Do you want to see your wildest dreams come to life? Do you want all your plans to succeed?

If this is what you want, then begin by setting your God free. Don't condemn the awesome King of the universe to a dull existence in a box. Let God be God and He'll let you be you.

CHAPTER 45

The Real Jesus

*I*f our view of God is twisted, our relationships with people, made in His image, will be equally distorted. If we want pure and loving friendships, we need a God who is our friend. We need an image of God that is pure and clear and filled with light and love.

This perfect image is Jesus. "He is the image of the invisible God" (Colossians 1:15). He is the "friend who sticks closer than a brother" (Proverbs 18:24). Tragically, many Christians are afraid of Jesus. They want to feel His pure, safe love, but for some reason they cannot. Logically they know that their faith shields them from all judgment and that "there is no fear in love. But perfect love drives out fear" (1 John 4:18). Yet they have trouble experiencing this reality. They feel strangely aloof from Jesus and can never relax with Him.

Their problem is that they are letting a false Jesus obstruct their vision of the true One. An idol stands in the way, and this idol must be destroyed. Idols do not just go away. They must be torn down, deliberately, savagely, with our bare hands. Most Christians are loathe to do this with an idol who bears the name of Jesus. That Jesus-idol may have kept them for years in chains of fear and unreality, yet still they refuse to do away with him just because his name happens to be Jesus. Does this Jesus love them? No, he cannot; he is an idol. This Jesus deserves to be crucified.

Here in North America our greatest idol is the false Jesus. Our god is Jesus as he might have been had he never faced death on the cross but instead had simply grown old. We have a tired Jesus, a bald and toothless Jesus, a Jesus with sagging jowls who, far from conquering death, has struck a workable compromise with the dark powers of this world. At the other extreme we opt for a Superman Jesus so far removed from our ordinary lives that we cannot relate to Him. Isn't it high time these impostors were run out of town?

Paul refers to the false Jesus when he writes, "If someone comes to you and preaches a Jesus other than the Jesus we preached…you put up with it easily enough" (2 Corinthians 11:4). Even Jesus had to resist the temptation to be false to Himself. There was a Jesus who might have seized political power, who might have played the big shot by turning stones into bread, who might have swelled with pride at the sound of his own preaching, who might have controlled people's wills, who could easily have refused the way of the cross, or who in many other ways could have worshiped the devil rather than the living God. To this false Jesus the true Jesus had to say, "No, that is not who I am."

Did you know that it is possible to idolize even Jesus? You do this whenever you place yourself out of His reach—either above Him in intellectual pride, or too far beneath Him in cringing self-abasement. Do you have a phony Jesus who should be put to death? This is hard to do. In our superficially Christian culture, the false

Jesus is slippery and subtle and wields staggering power. But listen to Isaiah: "Your ears will hear a voice behind you, saying, 'This is the way; walk in it.' Then you will defile your idols overlaid with silver and your images covered with gold; you will throw them away like a menstrual cloth and say to them, 'Away with you!'" (30:21-22).

Why not do this right now? Recall some time when you know you have been with the real Jesus, when His beautiful, loving voice has melted your heart. Then, in the presence of the true, take that false and fearful Jesus and throw him away. Do whatever you must do to banish this impostor, to let both him and yourself know for certain that never again will you be terrorized by the mere name of Jesus.

Finally, dedicate yourself wholeheartedly to the true Son of God. You will know Him by His perfect naturalness, by His approachableness, by His tender and healing presence. You will know Him by the way He connects you with pure love. Accept no substitute. Look into the eyes of the warm and loving friend of sinners, and promise that from now on you will keep yourself only for Him. "Taste and see that the LORD is good" (Psalm 34:8). Discover the God who is pure goodness, and then your whole path will be strewn with flowers.

CHAPTER 46

Let People
Be People

Letting God be Himself so that you too can be yourself is the first step to a life of love. The next step, which follows naturally, is to let other people be themselves. Isaiah's metaphor of the potter and the clay applies just as much to our relationships with people as it does to our relationship with God. Will you, a mere pot, presume to tell the Potter what He can and cannot do? In the same way, will you dare to lay a hand on one of His creations? Does one mug in your cupboard say to another mug, "I don't like the way you're made"? Does one broken shard lying in the dirt say to another broken shard, "Here, let me fix you up"?

If you want to be free, set others free. Give everybody lots of rope, even if they try to use it to hang you. Set people free to complicate your life, embarrass you, affront your standards, step on your toes. Don't be a doormat, but neither be scandalized when people act human. The more you reel others in and try to squeeze them into your mold, the less you'll enjoy them. To love people is to enjoy them truly, warts and all. Give everyone the freedom to be imperfect. The American slaves were not set free because they were all jolly good fellows, but because they were human beings.

I used to be afraid of my daughter's temper tantrums. It wasn't the anger itself I feared so much as the broken relationship. When she stormed into her room and slammed the door, I was afraid of the time she would slam it forever. This fear persisted until one day I stood outside her door, as usual barricaded from within by her bookshelf, and rather than loudly demanding to be let in, I said quietly, "Heather, I understand what you're feeling." After a long silence, a tiny, plaintive voice replied, "You do?" And eventually the door was opened, for I had said the magic words. I had given my daughter complete freedom to hate me.

Do we long for our unbelieving friends to find freedom in Christ? First we must set them free to be unbelieving sinners. It is easy to give others the freedom to be kind and loving; the freedom we do not want to extend is the freedom to sin. But doesn't God Himself grant us this freedom? Astonishingly, He has given all of us full license to hate and reject Him, and to do so as fiercely, as deviously, or as politely as we choose. Before we go around accusing others of enslavement to sin, we ought to take stock of our own freedom. If we are truly free, then the freedom of others—even the freedom to sin—will be vastly important to us. We would much rather see people freely sinning than have them fall into the clutches of pious legalism.

Freedom is not a commodity to possess and keep all to ourselves. Like everything good, we have freedom only if we're continually bestowing it on others. The economy of God's kingdom collapses if the currency is not kept circulating. What do you want in life? Start giving it away and it will be yours.

This is the essence of the Golden Rule, "Do to others what you would have them do to you" (Matthew 7:12). Do you want your in-laws to accept you? Accept them! Do you long for a blessing from your father? Bless him! What do you lack? What do you want so badly you can taste it? Whatever it is, this is your precious gift for others. Give it away!

For forty years I thought that a gift had to be something I was good at, not something I was missing. Now I know that the fact that I think so much about love, and am constantly wondering how to do it, shows that this is my gift. Now I know that it is precisely people like me, the desperately lonely, who have the gift of intimacy.

You'll make more friends in two months by becoming interested in others than you can in two years by trying to get others interested in you. Consider the prayer of Saint Francis: "O Divine Master, grant that I may not so much seek to be consoled, as to console; to be understood, as to understand; to be loved, as to love. For it is in giving that we receive."

People do not want to be told how to live. They want to be loved. Lecturing, cajoling, and manipulating will only bring about a cynical attitude toward humanity. Even when others do happen to change under your influence, you will not respect them for it. If you want people to be human beings rather than puppets, take your hands off their strings. Give them plenty of room to breathe, and you'll breathe easier yourself.

I cannot set anyone else free. Only God can do that, and even He wants their cooperation. But if I make a habit of treating others as if they are already free, they'll stand a much better chance of getting the hang of it. The reason they are not kind and loving may well be that no one has ever treated them as if they are. If you want to see kingly qualities, treat people like kings.

CHAPTER 47

Kindness

S ome years ago my friend Bob Gemmell was wondering what his role was at church. He held no title or position and was never called on to minister publicly. Though very gifted, he had no sense of how to put his gifts to use in that particular setting. He wasn't sure whether he fit. Seeking the Lord on this question, Bob felt God say to him, "Just be kind to others. Not many people are kind these days."

It is easy to overmystify love. But really it's little more than a profound courtesy. We cannot produce an invisible mystery. But if we practice simple kindness from the heart, the mystical element will follow like divine wine poured into a waiting chalice.

One day I was feeling so glum that all I could do was sit and stare blankly at the wall. Outside it was raining, and after a while, as I listened to the splash of drops against the windowpane, there came to me the words of the old hymn "Little Things" by Julia Fletcher:

> Little drops of water, little grains of sand,
> Make the mighty ocean and the pleasant land.

When I was a child we used to sing this hymn in school assemblies. I had not thought of it for years, but remembering it now, the last verse especially spoke to me:

Little deeds of kindness, little words of love,
Help to make the Earth, like the heaven above.[7]

This is true. It is not great deeds but small ones that usher in the kingdom of heaven most powerfully. When one is perfectly content to have a life that is small and ordinary, then one's life becomes great.

That day I set about to perform some "little deeds of kindness" and to speak and write some "little words of love." I knew exactly what to do; there were many small deeds I had been putting off because I was too busy writing an important book! But from the moment I sat down to write a short note to a friend, my glumness vanished.

Kindness is not my strong suit. But over and over I've learned the power of small deeds of kindness for lifting depression. Kindness lifts depression because it strikes at the root of depression, which is self-condemnation. John teaches exactly this: "Dear children, let us not love with words or tongue but with actions and in truth. This then is how we know that we belong to the truth, and how we set our hearts at rest in his presence whenever our hearts condemn us" (1 John 3:18-20).

If your heart condemns you, start looking around for someone to love. How simple this is! But it works. Lovingkindness works better than anything else for clearing the conscience. It works, that is, unless you are the sort of person who is already so busy helping others that you neglect your own soul. It is no good adopting do-gooding as a surreptitious route to greatness. Flee from organized good! Rediscover the secret of small random acts of kindness—those mysterious little deeds that are so spontaneous that "your left hand [does not] know what your right hand is doing" (Matthew 6:3).

Kindness must be genuine. The deed must arise out of a palpable purity unmixed with any other motive. You will know the real thing because a restful, shining kindness will touch your own heart first, freeing you from any taint of the compulsiveness that so often accompanies good deeds. Pressure, anxiety, hurry—these are signs of performance, not kindness.

Kindness is one of the fruits of the Holy Spirit listed in Galatians 5:22. Peter mentions it too in a similar list: "Make every effort to add to your faith goodness; and to goodness, knowledge; and to knowledge, self-control; and to self-control, perseverance; and to perseverance, godliness; and to godliness, brotherly kindness; and to brotherly kindness, love" (2 Peter 1:5-7).

Probably there is a natural progression inherent in this list. For example, if you are presently growing in knowledge, it's likely you must soon progress to the next item on the list—self-control—in order to balance your pride. The crowning jewel of Peter's list is love, and it seems no accident that "brotherly kindness" immediately precedes this. Little deeds of kindness do indeed open the door to love.

Once we acknowledge that we do not love well, many of us get hung up on thinking that we do not know how. We say, "I do not know how to love so-and-so." But try asking the question, "What if I did know?" Use your imagination. What if you did know how to love that person? What sort of things would you say or do?

Anyone who is honest will readily see an answer to this question. For the truth is, we do know how to love. We just don't do it. In the Lord's Prayer we say, "Give us this day our daily bread." But what about our daily clay? What about the wonderful nourishment that can come only through a human touch, a human smile, a simple interaction with another person? Some people can have a marvelous time just going to the corner store; others would not be impressed if the whole world threw them a party. In the long run it does not matter whether other people are kind to us or nasty. What matters is whether we are kind to others.

No act of kindness is too small to be significant. After Jesus washed His disciples' feet He instructed them to imitate Him, saying, "Now that you know these things, you will be blessed if you do them" (John 13:17). What counts is not the act itself, but the purity of the heart behind it. When kindness does our own heart good, we can be sure it will bless others, too. People need to be someone to someone else. Apart from relationships, we fade out and begin to forget who we are. Being remembered by another, even in the homeliest of ways, can bring us back to ourselves.

Therefore: Send flowers to that angry, rebellious daughter. Write letters to that brother who never answers. Pick up the phone and call that elderly parent whose light is so dim it is almost extinguished. Do not be satisfied with loving people in your own mind. Love them until they feel your love.

CHAPTER 48

Intercession

*P*rayer is a primary means of practicing the presence of people. Indeed this is precisely what prayer is. In prayer to God, we lovingly practice the divine personhood of the Father, the Son, the Holy Spirit, or all three together. In contemplating the Trinity, we contemplate the mystery of relationship itself, of perfect love. In doing so we ourselves enter into this perfect relationship and so "participate in the divine nature" (2 Peter 1:4).

Similarly, praying for other people begins with entering into a deep love relationship with those people, no matter who they are. Jesus said, "Love your enemies,...bless those who curse you, pray for those who mistreat you" (Luke 6:27-28). If we cannot honestly bless others, we are not yet ready for intercessory prayer. Our prayers then should be for ourselves, not for anyone else. Without love we have nothing to pray. Without love we cannot pray according to God's will, for His will is love. Many people ask, "What is God's will for my life?" when instead they should ask, "Where is God's love in my life?"

Once I was praying for a neighbor who was in the habit of playing loud music late at night. "Lord," I prayed, "please find that fellow something else to do." Suddenly the Lord interrupted my prayer to say, "Don't pray for anyone you do not love. If you cannot love him, save your breath." I have never forgotten this. It changed my prayer life. I needed to love that neighbor, and that was all I needed. This was the answer to my prayer.

Much of what goes by the name of intercessory prayer is not true intercession at all, but judgment. People pass judgment on others and then use prayer to try to get God to reinforce those judgments. We use our own standards to decide what others ought to be like and how they should change, and then we pray, "Lord, please change these people so that they'll be more like me." Once people have conformed to our standards, then (i.e., never) we will love them.

This is entirely backward. We need to love people first, unconditionally, and only then will we know how to pray for them. True intercessors know that they can do nothing to change anyone else. Only God changes people. Knowing this, intercessors abandon all need to exercise influence over others, and out of this abandonment true prayer is born.

If we wish to pray effectively for others, we will never hold their faults against them, never reject them for their failings. It is not that intercessors are unaware of people's faults—but they are even more aware of the real person beneath the faults, the perfect child of God inside the rough exterior, and this is the person they choose to relate to and pray for. They pray not so much for the outer shell to be corrected, but rather for the spirit within to be encouraged and strengthened. If change is to happen, it will happen from the inside out. People do not change when their knuckles are rapped but when their inner beings are flooded with light.

Knuckle-rapping prayer is destructive, both for the intercessor and the intercessee. Both are deeply affected because such prayer emanates from an unhealthy relationship. To pray for other people without truly loving them is to engage in a kind of whining psychic manipulation. The term "charismatic witchcraft," used in some circles to describe such prayer, is not too strong. One might as well be sticking pins into a doll.

Not all phony intercession is charismatic witchcraft; much of it is a groping after love. This groping prayer is perfectly valid, indeed essential. But it is not intercession. True intercession begins with love. The same is true of worship. Much of what we call worship is really a searching after love for God. As vital and important as this is, it is not worship. Our Christianity would be more real and enjoyable if we would cultivate the habit of calling things what they are. Then, without guilt or pretense, we could relax and let ourselves be human. It takes a human to pray for another human. Even God became human in order to intercede for humanity.

Intercession is really no more than loving people in prayer. It means setting their faces before us and sitting in their presence, still and quiet, for long enough to find out who they are and what they need—in short, for long enough to love them. In prayer meetings one often hears the words, "Lord, we lift up so-and-so before You." As a formula this can grow tiresome; nevertheless it is exactly what we are to do. In our hearts we lift up people before the Lord, setting them above ourselves, above and beyond all our personal opinions and prejudices. We lift up people to God in order to see them not with our eyes but with His. Without this divine perception, we cannot pray rightly. We cannot bless others until we see them as God created them to be, pure and blameless.

Of course it is no good lifting up people in prayer only to put them down in person. If we do not love people when we are with them, we won't love them in our prayers either. All our fine prayers will fall to the ground if we cannot simply be with people in such a way as to bless them. If our presence does not bless, our prayers will curse.

Do we realize how closely linked are the spiritual and the social lives? As Agnes Sanford wrote, "The success of prayer depends as much on the depth of our love to man as on the height of our love to God." True intercessory prayer flows out of a loving relationship. It begins when we love people enough that we no longer need them to be any different than they are. Accepting and celebrating who they are, we can then encourage and bless all that they are becoming.

CHAPTER 49

The Thought Life

*P*rayer is inextricably entangled with our thinking. "Our thoughts spoil everything," wrote Brother Lawrence. "All the trouble begins with them. But we must be careful to reject them as soon as we perceive they are not necessary to what we are doing at the time." He went on to confess that "in the beginning he had often spent the entire time allotted to prayer in resisting his thoughts and then relapsing into them."[8]

All of us encounter this difficulty in prayer. But have we considered how this same obstacle crops up in our relationships with people? Wrapped in a fog of our own clamorous thoughts, we seldom achieve the inner quietness necessary to encounter others as they are. Whether alone or in company, our heads tend to be peopled with phantom beings with whom we carry on imaginary conversations rather than with real people. Even when face to face with another person, how often do we catch ourselves listening not so much to the other's thoughts as to our own? Nothing is more destructive of a living relationship than this habit of always trying to think of what to say next.

I used to keep an entire department of my brain busy dreaming up clever dialogues, all of which had but one motive: to exalt myself and belittle others. I poured endless time and mental energy into planning all that I would say and do to make myself look good and others foolish. Thank God He granted me grace to renounce this futile thinking! Gradually I'm learning that the best way to present myself is to become present to others, and that the most powerful form of influence is to empty myself and encounter others as they are.

Instead of wasting our solitude on imaginary mental conversations with people, we should pray for them. Instead of talking to people who are not there, we should talk to the God who is. Much of the battle for love takes place in the mind. "The mind of sinful man is death, but the mind controlled by the Spirit is life and peace" (Romans 8:6).

Do you let the Holy Spirit control your thoughts? Or does your thinking control you? Are you ruled by an unquiet mind? In Western civilization we've fallen prey to an excessive rationalism. We think about everything far too much. There's nothing wrong with thinking, except that so much of ours is tainted with anxiety and control. Far from drawing us nearer to God or to one another, the restless activity of our minds tends to keep us one step removed from reality.

Learning how to love takes vigilance, dedication, work. What makes us think we can get away without doing this work? The New Testament is full of exhortations concerning it. Many Christians are eager and willing to do all kinds of "work for the Lord," but somehow the fundamental work of learning how to love gets overlooked. We languish in bad habits of thinking, begging God to help us and wondering why He does not, when really what is needed is a little mental discipline. We must "take captive every thought to make it obedient to Christ" (2 Corinthians 10:5). We think all the time anyway—why not resolve to think only good thoughts? While self-effort alone is never sufficient, God is always eager to reward the smallest steps taken trustfully in this direction.

James taught us how to think when he wrote, "The wisdom that comes from heaven is first of all pure; then peace-loving, considerate, submissive, full of mercy and good fruit, impartial and sincere" (3:17). Notice that these are relational qualities. To James the test of good thinking is not how intellectually sound and rigorous it is, but whether it leads to warmth and intimacy with others. In this passage he contrasts "the wisdom that comes from heaven" with another sort of "wisdom" characterized by "envy and selfish ambition," which "does not come down from heaven but is earthly, unspiritual, of the devil" (3:15-16).

It is not difficult to discern between these two types of thinking. What is difficult is to submit all of our thoughts to James's standards of perfect purity and peace and to act accordingly. Yet short of doing this, we cannot grow in love, for love is "first of all pure; then peace-loving." Therefore, start saying no to any thought tainted by impurity or anxiety, and dedicate your mind instead to the wholly pure, the wholly peaceful. Feel the relief that comes when you give yourself permission to think this way. Get enough relief happening in your life, and you will fill up with the love of God. God's love will come riding toward you on waves of relief.

CHAPTER 50

Will

Having considered the mind, we turn now to a deeper level of our being: the will. This is important because love is not a thought or a feeling but a decision, an act of the will.

To know whether you truly love, it is not enough to examine your feelings. Rather you must look at your will to see which way it is pointing. If the needle on a compass points north, it doesn't mean you have reached your destination. But it does mean you can be sure of your direction. In the same way, when you point your will in the right direction, you may not immediately feel good. But if you keep moving in that direction, good feelings will inevitably follow.

Often there is a delay between the making of a right choice and the arrival of peace and joy. But in a person who is honestly seeking God and His love, this delay is not long. Usually it's just long enough to ensure that the decision that has been made is firm enough to stand against future opposition.

Jesus said, "If you obey my commands, you will remain in my love.... I have told you this so that my joy may be in you and that your joy may be complete" (John 15:10-11). Jesus wants us to have complete joy. It is ours for the taking, but not without the making of some hard choices. Jesus' commands, since they accord with our true nature, are not burdensome but freeing. Nevertheless they are still commands, and if we want the benefits of complete joy and love we must listen to the voice of the Good Shepherd and do what He says.

This is where the word *practice* comes in. This is the part of the spiritual life that *we do*. Divine virtues are offered to us, but they will never become ours until we practice them. Many Christians are waiting around for God to do something for them that He is never going to do—because He has already done it! Nothing is ours unless we make it ours. If we want something, our will must awaken and claim it. Often this happens best in adversity. The time when practice must do its work is when a gift or a grace we thought was ours seems suddenly taken away. By continuing to practice grace in its apparent absence, virtue is worked into our will in such a way that henceforth we'll always have it.

Hearing the word *will*, we may think of setting our faces like flint and screwing up our courage. But this is not the way the will works. In a godly person the will operates through humble submission. A hardened will is tough and crusty, but the will of a lover is soft, pliable, silky, organic. There's a saying that the heart is like a parachute: It works only when it's open. The will, too, is made for opening, accepting, receiving. The essential operation of the will is to lay itself down.

When everything around us looks dark and wrong, when all our circumstances combine to lure us toward rage or confusion or despair, still something stirs deep inside, something like a flower petal, bright and gentle and unlikely, catching our eye, drawing us, until we find ourselves relaxing our hold on our destiny, giving up all need to control and saying once again, "Yes, I will trust. One more time, I will let go." This is the proper use of the will.

No part of the Christian life is harder than this continual submission of the will. All the rest of the world operates in the opposite way, using will power to assert its rights and achieve what it wants. Why shouldn't Christians, too, entrench themselves in ego and reap all the benefits of self-aggrandizement? But Jesus showed a different way when He taught us to pray, "Not my will, but Thine be done."

Nothing is more powerful than the right exercise of the will in the midst of adversity. This is faith. Faith is not just belief in a body of doctrine. Faith is making good choices in bad circumstances. Without such testing, our wills would remain lazy, indecisive, unpracticed. Only with practice are good habits formed. A habit of loving God and people can be acquired. It will not happen magically. We must apply our wills over and over in tough situations in order to acquire virtue.

Without divine grace, of course, we could do nothing. But whether we're aware of it or not, God's grace is *always* present. He is always helping, blessing, pouring out love and gifts without limit. God is always doing His part. The only question is: Am I doing mine?

Love is both a noun and a verb. In its noun form, love is everywhere, all around, ever present. It's as though we lived in an immense field of beautiful flowers filled with nectar. But the nectar must be extracted to make honey; the bee must come and do its work. Love must become a verb.

Brother Lawrence expressed it this way: "We are to be pitied for our willingness to be satisfied with so little. God has infinite treasures to give us, and we are satisfied with a brief passing moment of piety. By our blindness we restrain the hand of God and so stop the flow of the abundance of His graces. But when He finds a soul imbued with a living faith, He pours into it His graces without limit. It is like a torrent forcibly diverted from its usual course, which having found a passage pours through irresistibly in an overwhelming flood."[9]

Will Rogers put it even more simply: "A man is about as happy as he makes up his mind to be."

How much love do you want? It's your choice.

CHAPTER 51

Choice

The world is not well, but living well means accepting life for what it is. More than just accepting our existence in this vale of tears, we should freely choose life—hard and bright, glorious and painful, large and overwhelming as it is. Archimedes said, "Give me a place to stand and I will move the world." This is that place: free choice. We should not just accept our troubles but choose them. We should say, "Yes, I choose this particular problem or pain because I know it is perfectly designed for the advancement of my soul."

Most of us never really accept the conditions of life in a fallen world. When troubles arise, our automatic response is to reject our life, or at least its unsavory aspects, as if it were possible to separate ourselves from what is actually happening. "No, no," we say, "this cannot be the way things really are. This ugly business cannot be happening to me."

But guess what? This *is* happening to you. You *are* one hundred thousand dollars in debt. You *do* work at a job you hate, and your boss *does* think you're a jerk. As much as you'd like to be healthy, you *do* have the flu, or cancer, or AIDS. Your marriage *is* a mess, and you *do* have a shifty-eyed son and a daughter on drugs. This very moment you may be on your way to somewhere you do not want to go with someone you do not want to be with. And on and on it goes.

If these are not your problems, then you have other ones. Make your own list. Everyone has problems. What varies is how they are handled. You may need to take action to change something, but before you can change anything, you must first acknowledge it. Pretending it isn't there or wishing it away won't work. As John Lennon put it, "Life is what happens to you while you're making other plans."

God did not reject the world because of its messiness. He didn't turn away in disgust, deeming Himself too pure to get involved. Instead He rolled up His sleeves and entered the fray. "God so loved the world that he gave his one and only Son" (John 3:16). Accepting us wholeheartedly while we were still sinners, Jesus stuck His foot in the world's door like a salesman insisting on giving us a personal demonstration of His product: unconditional love. Yes, He wants everyone to buy; He really does intend to change the world. But His strategy is to do so by first embracing it.

We must do the same. Especially when it comes to the difficult people in our life, we must not merely accept them but choose them. The freedom to love comes only through deliberate choice. We are creatures of free will, and there is no other route to freedom except by exercising our will to choose. Willed freedom is the only freedom there is.

Marathon runners speak of "hitting the wall." Often encountered around the twenty-mile mark, the wall is a phase of excruciating pain during which the runner feels sorely tempted to give up. By pushing through the wall, runners learn to expand their pain threshold and so overcome all obstacles. They choose their pain in the form of running, but the effect of making hard choices in this discipline carries over into other areas. "Everything I know about life," observed one marathoner, "I learned at the wall."

Sooner or later every human relationship comes to the wall. To choose the pain of involvement with others, rather than merely enduring it, is empowering. To choose the difficult people in one's life is the beginning of love. If we feel we cannot love such people, it is because we have never chosen them. At one time, perhaps, we actually invited these people to share our journey. But we never expected them to take over so completely! The person we once naively chose was not the monster who now stands before us.

In certain relationships we may feel we no longer have any choice. This is a lie. Even with people we never deliberately chose—such as our parents—still a choice is open to us. Our choice is to accept or to reject, to love or to hate.

People like to be chosen, and when we choose them, often they will feel this change in our attitude. Choice need not take the form of licking boots or selling one's soul. God had a "chosen people," but it didn't mean He was easy on them! Nor did He choose them because of their wonderful, warm qualities. No, it was His choice alone that ennobled them. The choosing demonstrated that God was in the driver's seat, taking the initiative, acting rather than reacting.

Choice empowers the chooser. Jesus hung on the cross not because anyone forced Him but because He chose it. He chose it because His faith was in something larger than suffering. If you cannot get your arms around your suffering, how will you ever get your arms around the something larger? Embrace your painful relationships. They are a part of your life, the only life you have.

Rejection and hate will never change things. But listen: You can change anything through love.

CHAPTER 52

Practical Hope

When you cannot seem to love people, you can still have hope. For "these three remain: faith, hope and love. But the greatest of these is love" (1 Corinthians 13:13).

One day while considering this verse, it struck me that there is a progressive order to these three words. If love is the greatest of the three, then hope is the second greatest and faith the third.

Like many believers, for years I put much more stock in faith than in love. Theologically I would have admitted the preeminence of love, but in practice I worked harder at faith. As for hope, I hardly knew what that was. When I realized that the order of these things is opposite to what I had thought and lived, it stopped me in my tracks.

I found this insight reinforced by a sentence in Brother Lawrence's writings: "All things are possible to him who believes, more to him who hopes, still more to him who loves, and most of all to him who perseveres in the practice of these three virtues."[10]

What could it possibly mean, I wondered, that hope could

accomplish more than faith? Faith could move mountains. What then might hope do?

Pondering this, it gradually changed the way I looked at people. The center of gravity in my relationships shifted. Before this I had always wanted to change people. Now I began to wonder what changes I had to make in myself in order to serve others.

As a Christian I had always wanted to fix people. I wanted to win them to Christ, proclaim the gospel, heal diseases, and generally shake the troops—to say nothing of getting people to like me! After years of striving, however, I realized that all my efforts were not accomplishing these ends. I had faith—or so I thought. What then was missing?

Hope and love were missing. If they were present at all, they were not in first place. I had laudable ends in mind, but the means were all wrong. Faith, I came to see, is a lesser thing than hope and love, because it has more to do with ends than with means. When I have faith it tends to be *for* something; I have some end in sight. But hope is more nebulous. If faith is a candle in the night, then hope is an anchor buried in the depths of the sea. Hosea prophesied that the "door of hope" would be found in "the Valley of Achor" (2:15)—that is, in the pit of desolation.

"Faith is being sure of what we hope for" (Hebrews 11:1), but hope is not sure—it is only hope. The nebulousness of hope sets it apart as a more precious thing than faith. Hope's softer focus makes it more people-friendly. While it is possible to hope for certain ends to be accomplished in others' lives, this is not biblical hope. Biblical hope is placed in the God who loves people. I may hope that Jack becomes a Christian, but whether he does or he doesn't, can I still trust him to God? If not, then even if he does become a Christian, it will not improve our relationship. I will only find there is something else wrong with him that needs fixing.

Hope in people begins with hope in God. Hope is a deep, quiet trust in the God-created souls of others. Free of manipulation, hope attaches no strings, makes no demands. To make demands on others is really to make demands on oneself. Demandingness puts one's whole being under tremendous strain, but hope lets go of this load. Letting go is the beginning of hope, and hope is the beginning of service.

While the three virtues of faith, hope, and love work best in combination, the power of hope alone should not be underestimated. Godly hope, in the devil's eyes, is poison. It's the one spot of health showing up on the cancerous x-ray of Satan's plans for the perfect reign of terror. If there is one ray of hope in a troubled marriage, then there is everything. No spiritual gift can save a marriage, but hope can save it. No amount of faith can produce healthy, joyful friendships. But hope and love will do the trick.

CHAPTER 53

Sacrifice

All progress in the Christian life comes through sacrifice. Always something must be given up in order that something better might be gained.

When faced with difficulties, I often picture my life as a voyage in a hot-air balloon. As the balloon sinks toward earth, what ballast must I throw out in order to gain altitude? What is weighing me down? What must I give up in order to rise above my struggles? Whenever I feel burdened there is something to which I cling. Let it go and my soul will soar.

Similarly when problems arise with people, I can ask: What must I give up in order to make this relationship work? Sometimes the relationship itself must be sacrificed or allowed to assume a different form. More often I must give up my need to control, my refusal to forgive or to offer apology, or my reluctance to face an awkward confrontation. In any case, I need never remain trapped or wallow in despair. I take it as an axiom that I can always do something to gain altitude.

This is the mark of the believer in the gospel. The true Christian believes in freedom, total freedom in all circumstances, because "it is for freedom that Christ has set us free" (Galatians 5:1). When Jesus accused the Jews of being slaves, they wouldn't believe it. "Oh yes, you are!" Jesus insisted. "Everyone who sins is a slave to sin.... If the Son sets you free, you will be free indeed" (John 8:33-36).

Religious slaves do not admit their slavery. They may think they are free, but they are not free indeed. They cling to an idea of freedom without the experiential reality. Stuck in their ruts, they will not concede there is any answer to their problems. If you challenge them they will say, "No, this is just the way life is. Nothing can be done about it." The more you push them, the more they'll deny any problem. Many are trapped this way in jobs, in marriages, in unhealthy relationships, in bad habits, in neurotic illnesses. They are not free because they do not believe there is any way out.

The believer in the gospel knows that there is always a way out. Moreover, this way out can be found and taken right now, today. "Now is the time of God's favor, now is the day of salvation" (2 Corinthians 6:2). What keeps people from finding the way out? The cost of sacrifice. Counting this cost, they balk. It seems preferable to stay stuck. The price of freedom is too high. Sacrifice is odious.

Whenever I feel stuck in a relationship, I remind myself that I am here on earth to learn how to love. I take it for granted that there is some way to love every person, not dutifully and artificially, but with a pure, sincere love. What is this way? It is not always obvious. To learn such love, it is usually necessary to be locked inside a room from which there is no other exit except love. Love is the one answer to everything. Love is the only way to be free.

Therefore in every relationship I become willing to sacrifice anything in order to be free. I make no exceptions. I do not have a category for people I cannot love. The moment I allow such a category, I inhibit my own freedom. According to Proverbs 17:19, "He who builds a high gate invites destruction." So I build walls against no one. I make a point of keeping all gates open, whatever the cost. I do not worry about the other person's gate; I focus on opening my own. By personally accepting total responsibility, I achieve total freedom.

Of course, the gate I keep open is the gate of my heart, not necessarily the gate of my house. I am no doormat for abusers and troublemakers. I recognize that not everyone is my friend and that enemies require appropriate handling. Many people do not even realize they have enemies. They would not know an enemy if one came up and hit them on the head. Why else do so many remain in abusive relationships?

Love is not necessarily support, politeness, or hospitality. Some people are better loved at a distance! In these cases, I must sacrifice my arrogance in thinking I can keep everybody happy and be all things to all people. Humbly I accept my limitations, knowing that true freedom functions within boundaries. With David I can say, "The boundary lines have fallen for me in pleasant places" (Psalm 16:6). The way of sacrifice is pragmatic, realistic. My greatest sacrifice is to accept my human limitations and to live within them.

CHAPTER 54

The Door

*P*ractice must be practical. It doesn't matter how good something looks; if it doesn't work, it's not practical. In relationships, the practical way is the one that works, the one that actually brings people closer together.

Therefore do what works with people, not what doesn't work. If one angle isn't paying off, try something different. Never give up.

How many give up on God because they insist on relating to Him in a way that doesn't work? When their efforts to be spiritual do not produce true spirituality, they get angry, slam the door, and go home. They give up on prayer because they will not look for it in the most obvious place of all—right under their noses. Prayer cannot be forced; it's the most natural of all activities. Prayer is like one's own fingerprints. You cannot have someone else's prayer life; you can only have your own.

In the same way, we often give up on finding intimacy with other people because we will not accept them as they are. When I go to the house of my friend, I must enter through the door. If I try to go down the chimney, I'll get stuck. If I march headlong into a wall, I'll hurt myself. It's no good cursing my friend for the bump on my head and saying, "That so-and-so should have put a door in this wall."

Our goal is to come into the presence of others and to make ourselves present to them. Many relationships fail because we are too stubborn to walk around to the front of the house and enter through the door. True, the door may be narrow, yet still it is the proper and by far the easiest means of access. Even Jesus submits to entering our lives by the door. He said, "I tell you the truth, the man who does not enter the sheep pen by the gate, but climbs in by some other way, is a thief and a robber" (John 10:1).

Every relationship has doors, windows, and walls. Practice entering through the doors, and then the walls, far from presenting an obstacle, will be a source of warmth and security.

Where is the door in the house of your marriage? Maybe it's in the kitchen. Many a marriage would be renewed if the husband would spend some time visiting with his wife while she prepares a meal. Better still, let the husband prepare the meal, or let them work together. Zechariah prophesied that "every pot in Jerusalem and Judah will be holy to the LORD Almighty" (14:21). Are the pots in your house holy? Are they instruments to bring about intimacy? When even your pots are glorious, how much more glorious will be those who use them!

Brother Lawrence is known as the "kitchen saint" because he actually experienced more of God's presence in the kitchen than in his formal times of prayer. "He found that the best way of reaching God was by doing ordinary tasks entirely for His love," and "that it was a great delusion to think that time set aside for prayer should be different from other times, for we were equally obliged to be united to God by work in the time assigned to work as by prayer during prayer time."[11]

Brother Lawrence abolished the hierarchy of activities. He silenced that snooty little voice that tells us that some things are more important than others. If this were really the case, it would follow that the less important things should be treated with relative contempt. This voice argues, for example, that to be forced to wait at a stoplight is beneath our dignity, and therefore in such a setting we are perfectly justified to become bored and impatient. When we give this voice full sway, we end up living our whole lives in boredom, impatience, and eventual despair. To exalt one part of life over another is to devalue ourselves and cheapen the human spirit.

When it comes to people, do you exalt some and treat others with contempt? No doubt you know people who behave like long stoplights. You're impatient for them to change, and when they don't, you feel justified being angry with them. Where is the door into these strained relationships? Often it lies in something ordinary: a small gift, a compliment, an act of service, a hand on the shoulder. Sometimes it is simply a matter of listening to the sound of the other's voice, unique in all the world. What color are his eyes? What is that one unforgettable mannerism she has? Become humble enough to notice these things, to enjoy and cherish them, and travel along them into the other's heart.

Will you make it your goal to come into the presence of each person you meet? If you want to go to Los Angeles, then get on a road that leads there. Countless people pour hours, whole lifetimes, into beliefs and practices that do not actually get them where they want to go. Spirituality must be practical. If it isn't actually producing more and more happiness, more and more freedom, and deeper and deeper love on a daily basis, then it's not the real thing.

If your relational style isn't working today, it won't work tomorrow either. Give it up, and replace it with something practical. This is the essence of practice. Find out what works in relationships, and do it.

FRIENDSHIP

*Every book is, in an intimate sense, a circular letter
to the friends of him who writes it.*

ROBERT LOUIS STEVENSON

So far in this book I have written a good deal about love. But now we come to the highest expression of love, which is friendship. God loves everyone, but only a few are His friends. Being a friend of Jesus is a higher calling than being a disciple. In Acts 11:26 we learn that the term *Christian* was what outsiders first labeled the believers. But Jesus' name for us is found in John 15:15: "I have called you friends." Friendship was Jesus' great dream for His church. He wanted to create a fellowship of friends such as the world had never seen. This would be His greatest miracle. Then "all men will know that you are my disciples, if you love one another" (John 13:35).

Years ago I opened a fortune cookie and read, "You will have many friends." As I had no friends at the time (or at least felt I had none), this struck me as a promise from God. I put this tiny piece of paper into my wallet and carried it around until the day it came true. Then I passed it on to a friend who needed it.

I still remember the day I realized that this promise had been fulfilled in my life. It happened in the twinkling of an eye. One day I had no friends, and the next day I had more friends than I could easily count. Something amazing happened to me. What was it?

Although I had been a Christian for many years, when I say I had no friends, I mean that seriously. As a writer, an introvert, a contemplative, I had limited time for people. Yes, there was my family. I had a good marriage and a daughter I loved, but beyond this small circle my relationships were shallow. I do not mean that my conversations never got beyond the weather. No, I had many meaningful interactions with people. But at some deep level that I tried to ignore,

I did not feel connected. I had many contacts, but no real community.

Even if I did connect with someone, the moment that person was out of sight I would break the connection. Something in me broke it, as if somehow I had learned that it was not safe to get too close to people. I could have moved to the other side of the world without a twinge of regret.

If I were to retrace all the steps in the process through which I emerged from this prison, I would have to write another book. Yet in a sense, the change I experienced was simple and did happen overnight. If a traveler wants to get to New York and suddenly realizes he is heading in the wrong direction, all he has to do is turn around. He has not yet arrived at New York. He may still have a long journey ahead. But at least now he is not lost. He knows he is headed in the right direction, and this makes all the difference.

One incident marks the moment when I changed direction. It happened on my birthday, when my wife had invited some "friends" over for cake. Usually I like to spend my birthday quietly, but for once I grudgingly consented to a small party. Predictably I was out of sorts, in no mood to put on a happy face for company. Somehow I faked my way through a painful evening.

Toward the end, as we sat around in the living room, someone suggested that they pray for me. Bowing my head, I listened with a mixture of skepticism and vague hope to some very nice, very ordinary prayers for my well-being. As usual something inside me was already preparing to break any connection that might be formed with these people.

The prayer time came to an end, and nothing happened. At

least, I thought nothing had happened until I opened my eyes. Then, looking around that small circle of familiar faces, all at once they appeared strangely bright, luminously tender and present. For reasons I could not fathom, tears came to my eyes.

For some time there was silence. All eyes were upon me.

"What's going on?" asked my wife eventually. "What are you feeling?"

Still for some time I struggled in silence with my emotions.

Finally I took a deep breath and said, "I'm feeling that everyone here loves me."

Like a pebble cast into the ocean, this was a seemingly small event, yet its ripples turned into waves, and those waves are still rocking my foundations in a way that feels as gentle and wonderful as the rocking of a cradle.

John wrote, "This is love: not that we loved God, but that he loved us" (1 John 4:10). Whether with God or with people, receiving love is the key to friendship. For as I am loved, so shall I love.

It is one thing to believe that God loves me. But to believe that people love me too, and to receive their love as from God—in some ways this has come to me as an even greater revelation. As George MacDonald wrote to his wife, "Thank you for your precious love—the most precious thing I have: for I will not divide between the love of God directly to me and that which flows through you."[1]

Receivership

The way I learned to receive love reminds me of that strangest of all Jesus' parables, the one traditionally known as "the dishonest steward" (Luke 16:1-9). I never understood this story until I realized that it's about friendship. This interpretation is borne out by the moral Jesus Himself draws: "I tell you, use worldly wealth to gain friends for yourselves, so that when it is gone, you will be welcomed into eternal dwellings" (v. 9).

I like the suggestion that the road to heaven is paved with many friendships. As the parable opens, we see a man who has no real friends because he is powerful, self-reliant, and consumed with making money. He's also on the shady side, and when his indiscretions are finally uncovered, his master fires him. Suddenly life is not so rosy.

Listen to how this man thinks: "What shall I do now?" he moans. "My master is taking away my job. I'm not strong enough to dig, and I'm ashamed to beg.... I know what I'll do so that, when I lose my job here, people will welcome me into their homes" (vv. 3-4).

With bankruptcy staring this fellow in the face, he is forced to make some friends—fast. True to his nature, the way he does this involves yet another shady deal. Even so, "the master commended the dishonest manager because he had acted shrewdly" (v. 8).

This is confusing. At first the master was upset by his steward's dishonesty; later he commends him. What gives?

What gives is the man's self-reliance. In the master's eyes the real problem was the steward's arrogant independence—a bad trait in any employee. In the end the steward is smart enough to see his need of relying on other people. He is too proud to beg, but he's not too proud to accept charity from friends. He finds a way to receive.

Jesus makes it clear that this is a worldly tale. There's nothing spiritual here; the steward does not undergo a change of heart. He simply acts shrewdly in a tight fix. Finding himself in humble circumstances, he eats humble pie. Jesus' point is this: If the people of the world can humble themselves before others for practical reasons, how much more should the children of light show enough humility to make true friendships! Can we see that the purpose of money—as indeed of everything—is the making of friends?

Humility is knowing how to receive from others. Not surprisingly, one synonym for bankruptcy is *receivership*. All of us, in ourselves, are spiritually bankrupt. Like the dishonest steward we must face our bankruptcy and go into receivership. This is the *poverty of spirit* of the Beatitudes. To live this way is to be blessed. As spiritual bankrupts, we know that true riches are gained not through acquiring but through receiving. We know too that it is just as important to receive from people as to receive from God.

Only when we have learned how to receive do we become

capable of giving. The receiving must come first. It must come first because we are so proud. Everyone wants to give, but who except a bloodsucker wants to receive? Receiving in our society is regarded as low and selfish, the lot of beggars and weaklings. But just as "he who has been forgiven little loves little" (Luke 7:47), so the one who receives little will have little to give.

Many call themselves believers who are not receivers. They like good things, but they also like to be in control of how those good things come to them. This is not receiving but getting. Such people will take, but they will not accept. They will take anything except the risk of vulnerability, and so the mystery of friendship eludes them.

Then there are people so vulnerable that no matter what they are given, it is never enough. Jesus said, "Whoever has will be given more; whoever does not have, even what he has will be taken from him" (Mark 4:25). Chronic have-nots are in that condition because they cannot truly receive. Their hearts are like sieves, so that whatever anyone gives them immediately runs out. God continues to love these people, and so should we. But they cannot hold on to love. All the love in the world will do them no good until they learn to receive.

Believing is receiving.

CHAPTER 56

Safety

*H*ow did I come to feel safe enough with people to begin to receive their love? I think it happened because, around the same time, I was discovering safety with Jesus. I was making friends with Him.

For years I had believed in Jesus, worshiped Him, followed Him, even loved Him. But I had never felt we were friends. He was someone who kept me on edge, not someone with whom I could completely relax. Whenever I came to Him, I always felt bad for all the ways my life didn't measure up. Like Peter I would say in fear, "Go away from me, Lord; I am a sinful man!" (Luke 5:8). In a sense, instead of inviting Jesus into my life, I kept telling Him to go away. I knew I wasn't good enough for Him and never would be.

Of course I had the gospel all backward. Rather than coming to Jesus for acceptance and forgiveness, I thought I had to become acceptable before He would receive me. Theologically I knew this was wrong, but in practice I still behaved this way. I didn't know how to receive from God any more than I knew how to receive from people.

What a pitiful Catch-22! I was *saved* by Jesus, but I did not feel *safe* with Him. Indeed it is so common for Christians to speak of being *saved* that I wonder if this word may have outlived its usefulness. The best translation of John 10:9 reads, "I am the gate; whoever enters through me will be kept safe." Perhaps the word for our day is not *saved* but *safe*. Safety is what people crave, whether with God or with one another.

I did not feel safe with Jesus because He seemed too radical, too demanding, too holy. He said, "You are my friends if you do what I command" (John 15:14). To me this seemed too tall an order. Didn't Jesus want me to give to the poor, perform miracles, spread the gospel, and be ready to die for Him? I would have liked to do these things, but I couldn't. How could I serve anybody else when I was all wrapped up in myself? My big concern was just to lick depression in my life. When I died, I would be saved. But in this world, right now, I was not safe.

In this sad muddle, I had overlooked one fact: The law of Jesus is not what I cannot do but what I can. His commands, far from being too difficult for me, are in fact easy. "His commands are not burdensome" (1 John 5:3). Even the Old Testament states this clearly: "Now what I am commanding you today is not too difficult for you or beyond your reach.... No, the word is very near you; it is in your mouth and in your heart so you may obey it" (Deuteronomy 30:11,14).

In the New Testament Jesus says, "Come to me, all you who are weary and burdened, and I will give you rest.... For my yoke is easy and my burden is light" (Matthew 11:28,30). If I was not able to carry out the commands of Jesus, it was because I was not coming to Him for rest. Or for peace or joy or love or any other good thing. I was not receiving from Him, not letting Him be my friend.

Friends like to be with their friends. It wasn't until I realized that Jesus liked being with me, wreck though I was, and that He wasn't asking anything of me except to settle down and be comfortable with Him, that my nervous depression began to fade. Eventually I relaxed enough to hear one of Jesus' most important commands: "Do not be afraid." Always I'd been filled with terror by the verse, "If you love me, you will obey what I command" (John 14:15). But as I studied the context of this verse, I found that the two chapters surrounding it contain only five small commands: "Trust...in me" (14:1); "Do not let your hearts be troubled and do not be afraid" (14:27); "Remain in me" (15:4); and "Love each other" (15:12).

After this I began to see that the Bible's commands are not burdensome but healing and delightful. For example Psalm 37:3 reads, "Dwell in the land and enjoy safe pasture." Heeding this command of Jesus, how can I not let go of fear? Once my fears subside, I am ready to tackle anything. Feeling deep safety with God, I become ready to face any danger for Him.

To me the biggest danger had always been other people. But now I had something I was eager to share with others. I could never get excited about telling anyone how to be saved. But to discover that God is safe, warm, friendly, approachable, and that all He requires of His children is to relax and be ourselves—this is good news! Suddenly being a follower of Jesus became not at all out of reach but wonderfully doable.

Once we discover the good news, we want not only to tell others about it, but to act it out. As we have found Jesus to be safe, we in turn wish to be safe for others. We want people to feel safe enough with us to laugh and be silly, to let loose, talk crazily, cry, get angry, and confess sins. We want people to be free to be who they are, to find the healing of coming home, home to themselves.

What kind of people are safe to be around? People who are at home in their own skins. People free of guilt and moroseness, free of control and intensity and hidden agendas. Normal, natural people who know how to embrace others with love. Isn't this exactly the quality that is often missing from Christianity? "Love must be sincere" (Romans 12:9). Many Christians have tried every other kind of love except the sincere kind. But when we love others deeply, one paradoxical result is an acceptance of the surfaces people present, an ability to meet others where they are and enjoy them as they are. By practicing the presence of people, we become more present ourselves, more real and natural, and others are drawn to this.

Feeling safe in Jesus' friendship, we make others safe and we feel safe with them. We even learn to feel safe with dangerous people. Because we are committed to our own safety and the God of safety is with us, dangerous people cannot threaten or manipulate us as they once did. Instinctively we know how to handle them, when to keep clear, or when to break off a relationship entirely. If we're with a dangerous person, it's for a purpose, and we're in control. Rather than cringing, we take the initiative. Nothing can keep us from living safely. "You will not fear the terror of night, nor the arrow that flies by day" (Psalm 91:5).

I'm reminded of a Gary Larson cartoon that shows a monster

lying restlessly in a bed while a human being lurks underneath. Imagine—the devil cannot sleep at night because of the humans under his bed! For nothing is more dangerous than simple humanity—frank, open, naive, vulnerable. "When I am weak," wrote Paul, "then I am strong" (2 Corinthians 12:10).

CHAPTER 57

Chicken or Egg?

*I*f we know without doubt that Jesus is our friend, friendships with people will come easily. On the other hand, if we fear Jesus, we will fear everyone. Once I truly made friends with Jesus, I realized what a great many other friends I had too. In a sense nothing changed in any of my relationships. The change came in the form of an inner realization: I was blind, but now I could see, and what I saw was a host of friends who had been there all along. They were right in front of my eyes, but I hadn't seen them because my heart had been closed.

I wonder which came first—the chicken or the egg? Did I look into the face of Jesus, recognize Him as a friend, and so open up to human friendships? Or did I look into human faces, recognize and receive their love, and so draw nearer to Jesus?

My thesis in this book has been that these two events are so interconnected as to be one and the same. The one does not happen without the other. If we cannot find intimacy with human beings, we do not have intimacy with God either. We'll feel no closer to God than we do to the people around us. The quality of our spiritual life is best measured by the quality of our friendships. True growth will inevitably produce a new closeness to people, and if it does not, it's not the real thing.

To love God is to love people. In a sense it does not matter whether Jesus or some other person is the catalyst for this revelation. What matters is the revelation itself, the transforming change. What matters is that the heart opens up to give and to receive love.

Is anything more rare in this world than true friendship? In our mobile society, how common it is to think we have friends, only to discover that when circumstances change, loyalties change too. We need lasting friendships to keep us from being spiritually fickle and high-strung. Friends are like lightning rods. It's great to have a mountaintop experience with God, but if we're not well grounded in human relationships, the lightning on the mountain may fry us. Every lightning bolt from God must be grounded in the warm human eyes of a loved one.

Many Christians ardently seeking spiritual gifts and power would do much better to seek true friendships instead. No gift is more precious than a friend, and no power is greater than that released through the bond of brotherly love. My friend Laurie Hills says, "I have never sought God's unusual manifestations. His usual is fulfilling." Spirituality can be dangerous, but "love never fails" (1 Corinthians 13:8). To focus on anointing, on righteousness, on church, or on doing good—all of this may easily lead a person astray. But to focus on love will always keep one on the right path.

It is strange but true that the faces of our neighbors are often the faces of the big hairy monsters in our own closet. It's not that these people are ugly or nasty; probably they're as nice as we are. But we do not know how to relate to them in a way that is natural and life giving. Many Christians would rather look into their Bibles than into the eyes of a fellow human being. This is exactly what Jesus ran up against in the Pharisees. Many will pray, "Lord, I want to be close to You," yet never do anything to get close to the people around them. But God has designed it so that the route to Him lies through other people.

I may easily deceive myself that I love God. But do I love my family and friends? Those who regard themselves as godly—let their spouses and children and neighbors come forth and testify of their great and practical love for them!

Love is always particular. It is not a general, amorphous feeling. It finds its home in the heart of another person. The moment we assume we have learned how to love, we'll realize that we haven't yet loved *this* one. If love were a sport, then people would be the goalposts. It's not enough just to put on the uniform and run around the field kicking the ball. We need to score goals. We need to make real friendships. We must love in such a way as to light up another person's eyes. And then another and another and another.

Many people have become Christians only because someone loved them with a pure, safe, human love. When Paul sent Timothy to the Philippian church he commented, "I have no one else like him, who takes a genuine interest in your welfare. For everyone looks out for his own interests, not those of Jesus Christ" (2:20-21). Imagine—Paul knew of no one in Philippi except Timothy who had learned how to practice the presence of people!

What is required to build a fire? Paper, kindling, a match, and wood. Our paper is the Bible, the Word of God in Scripture. Our kindling is a broken and contrite heart, willing to be burned. The match is the Holy Spirit, without whom we are nothing. Yet even all this is not enough to get a good fire going. Paper and kindling burn up in no time, providing little heat. What we need, finally, is some good, solid firewood. We need one log resting up against another. We need the bond of friendship, of brotherly love.

CHAPTER 58

The Royal Law

"Every person I meet is like a star in my sky," my friend Daniel Adair tells me. "Whenever I meet someone new, I take that person and fix him or her in my heart. To do this, I literally see that person as a star, and I reach up and set that star in my sky. Where once was a patch of empty dark, there now blazes the living light of a soul I know and love. To set all people above me in this way helps me both to remember and to cherish them. When I'm lying alone in my bed at night, I look up into my sky and see all those stars, all the stars of everyone I've ever known, and one by one I remember them by name."

Isn't this exactly what the Lord does with His friends, calling each one by name and placing them in His heaven? Daniel's image reminds me of Psalm 19, which begins with a meditation on the glory of the heavens and goes on to a rapturous meditation on the goodness of God's law. Reading this psalm one day, it occurred to me that every word of praise applied to the law of the Lord could equally be applied to friendship. The middle section (vv. 7-11) could even be paraphrased as follows:

Friendship is perfect,
> reviving the soul.

Friends are trustworthy,
> making wise the simple.

Friendship is right, giving joy to the heart,
> and radiant, giving light to the eyes.

Friendship is so pure that it endures forever,
> so sure that it is altogether righteous.

Friends are more precious than gold,
> and sweeter than honey.

By our friends are we warned,
> and in keeping them there is great reward.

It should come as no surprise that friendship and divine law may be so easily interchanged. For friendship *is* the law of the Lord. This is "the royal law found in Scripture, 'Love your neighbor as yourself'" (James 2:8). Friendship is what love looks like when put into practice.

We know that the law of the Lord is "perfect," but can friendship really be described this way? Aren't friends full of human imperfections? Yes, but while friends are not perfect, friendship is. Friendship is the perfect bond of love between two imperfect people. Though we cannot be perfect in ourselves, we can be perfect *for* one another. You can be the perfect friend for me, and I for you.

Alone we are flawed, but in friendship even our flaws draw us together to make us strong. A character of Frederick Buechner's goes so far as to ask, "What's friendship, when all's done, but the giving and taking of wounds?"[2] It is the very perfection of the bond of friendship that enables all wounds to be sustained, turning every ill to ultimate good. When we were learning to walk, our parents were there to catch us when we fell. But who will catch us when we grow up? This is what friends are for.

This is also what the church is about. Ever wonder why the church is so flawed? Flaws form the best glue for friendship. Indeed a friendship without many shared failures will remain stilted and lame. We connect with others not primarily through our strengths, but through our weaknesses.

The church I attend has a motto: "Making Friendships That Count." Pastor Greg Schroeder once explained to me how this phrase came to him through studying Jesus' great prayer in John 17. Here Jesus begins by praying for Himself and His relationship with His Father; then He prays for His disciples; finally He prays for all future believers and for their relations with outsiders. Out of this prayer comes my church's focus on "making friendships that count: with God, with one another, and with the world."

Friendship is the proof of the gospel's pudding. It is the fulfillment of Jesus' prayer "that all of them may be one, Father, just as you are in me and I am in you" (John 17:21). The gospel is not just that God is for us or with us, but that He is *in* us and we are in Him, and therefore we can be in one another. Friendship is the practical expression of our mystical union in Christ. Hence in John's gospel the Great Commission to the church is not to go to the ends of the earth and make disciples, but to become the house of God by being friends with one another.

This too is the main thrust of all the letters of Paul. Great evangelist though he was, Paul never exhorted anyone (except Timothy) to be an evangelist. Rather he pleaded with the churches to lay down their internal struggles and to love each other. He said nothing to his people about taking the gospel to others, because they hadn't yet absorbed it themselves.

How important was friendship to Paul? Listen: "Now when I went to Troas to preach the gospel of Christ and found that the Lord had opened a door for me, I still had no peace of mind, because I did not find my brother Titus there. So I said good-bye to them and went on to Macedonia" (2 Corinthians 2:12-13). To Paul, in short, one friend was more important than all the converts who would be won through a great ministry that the Lord Himself was opening up! And Paul was right. A friend in the hand is worth a thousand in the bush. More to the point, Paul knew that the preaching of a man who sticks close to his friends is far more effective than the preaching of an isolated, overworked egoist. Perhaps Paul learned this lesson the hard way through his famous disagreement with Barnabus (see Acts 15:39)?

Jesus sent out His disciples two by two because He wanted His mission to be carried out by close friends working together. Friendship is not only the means but the end of the gospel. Friendship *is* the message Jesus wanted preached. Hence He prayed for us to be "brought to complete unity to let the world know that you sent me and have loved them even as you have loved me" (John 17:23). Neither our kind deeds nor our preaching best reveals Jesus to people, but rather the depth of our friendships. There are other ways through which the world may see Jesus, but without this one way, all others are in vain.

CHAPTER 59

A Penny Saved

Could it be that friendship is such a plain and homely thing that we do not even know what it is? Is this why, rather than giving friendship its place of first importance, we easily pass it by in favor of loftier pursuits?

I once had a dream that I was in a distant city, visiting with a group of strangers in a living room. These people struck me as a rather pitiful collection of plain, weak, colorless folk. I felt I was wasting my time among losers. Not until the end of the dream, just before waking up, did I realize that there was one thing about these people that was different from any other group I had ever been with: *They really loved each other.*

Here I had been in the presence of true friendship, and I hadn't even recognized it! In fact, I had scorned it.

Over the centuries many spiritual books have been written on love, but little has been written on friendship. The reason, I believe, is that church people generally know little about it. Compared to such great concerns as sound doctrine, evangelism, prayer, worship, and ministry, friendship does not seem so important. But the truth is that friendship is the foundation for all the rest. Without it the church will never accomplish her mission on earth.

In the 1960s I was a teenager. Back in those days I would never walk by a penny lying on the ground. A penny still had some value then. It was still worth bending down and picking one up, if only as a symbolic reminder that there was such a thing as good luck, that in this mundane world it was still possible to stumble upon hidden treasure.

Nowadays, I wouldn't stoop for a penny. I'd lower myself for a dime, maybe even for a nickel, but never for a penny. I wish I had a nickel for every penny I've walked by with my nose in the air. It's just not worth it anymore to pick one up. I wouldn't waste my time, energy, or dignity on such a trifle.

And yet here's the curious thing: *I still notice them.* It's not as if pennies are as common as dust. Worthless as they are, they're still worth noticing.

Isn't this something like our attitude toward love? Love is much more valuable than a penny. But isn't it also much more common? And don't we walk by it every day with our noses in the air? When a clerk in a store smiles at me, or when I pass a mother and her new baby on the sidewalk, or when I see a little old couple on a park bench in the autumn sunshine—do I allow these experiences to awaken love in me? Do I bend down, pick them up, and tuck them away in the pocket of my heart? Or have I become too busy and too important to stoop for love?

When I kiss my wife good-bye in the morning, is it a thoughtless ritual or is it love? Do I drink deeply, shallowly, or not at all from her eyes? Do I treat her as a penny, not worth my trouble, or is she a priceless treasure to me?

Do I regularly pass love by, not even seeing it for what it is?

Like air, love is all around us. Like the fruit in a bountiful orchard, it's ripe for the picking. There's no shortage of love. It's always right before our eyes in limitless supply. But we willfully blind ourselves to it, choosing to spend our lives getting on with more pressing matters. It's not that we do not notice love. We know it's there. But it's not important enough that we should humble ourselves to pick it up.

In fact, not only do we refuse to stoop for this penny, but we give it a wide berth and pass by on the other side of the road. It's almost as if the thing were radioactive or smelled bad. And so, inflating our lives with fool's gold, we devalue the currency of reality.

Why? Though we know love is not worthless like a penny, why do we treat it that way? Why don't we take the time to love?

Perhaps the question contains its own answer: time. We think love takes too much time. Noticing others, chatting, caring, giving of ourselves, doing good—all of this takes time. And isn't time our most precious commodity? Time is money. Time is of the essence. More time, more life. When we run out of time, we die.

Jesus said, "Greater love has no one than this, that he lay down his life for his friends" (John 15:13). Not many of us will literally be called on to spill our blood for our friends. Most often, the precious lifeblood we give to others will be in the form of our time and attention. These two go together. It is no good giving one without the other.

Can we afford this cost? If love is like money, in short supply, then the answer is no. If love is rare and expensive, then we cannot afford very much of it. But if love is like the air, there is no reason not to gather it freely and spend it as carelessly as breath.

The surprising truth is that love takes no time. Rather, love makes time. Love is the door into eternity. Wherever there is love the pressure of time fades away and eternal life floods in. A day spent with time nipping at one's heels is a futile, wasted day. But a day filled with love and friendship is a long, rich day in which even a penny becomes the treasure of kings.

CHAPTER 60

Jesus' Friends

Consider how important friendship was to Jesus. Obviously He enjoyed going to the home of His friends Mary, Martha, and Lazarus. This seems to have been a place where the Lord could unwind and feel like a normal human being. Jesus' disciples became His friends over time, but this little family, I suspect, had been His friends from youth. It's interesting that Lazarus was never called to be a disciple—at least not the sort of disciple who traveled with Jesus. He was merely Jesus' friend, and he stayed at home.

Mary and Martha, too, were homebodies. Other women traveled with Jesus and supplied all His needs, somehow feeding His large retinue even as He in turn fed the multitudes. But Martha and Mary were not like this. They stayed at home and met Jesus' needs in a different way, through friendship, homemaking, and prayer. They provided a place for Him to rest amid His travels and to be restored by the best food of all, homey companionship. How much Jesus must have appreciated Martha's warm and bustling hospitality!

Incidentally, Martha's busy-ness did not draw His famous rebuke of her, but rather her jealousy of Mary in saying, "Lord, don't you care that my sister has left me to do the work by myself? Tell her to help me!" (Luke 10:40). Generations of spiritual writers have seen in this story a commendation of contemplation over action. But it is quite possible to be bustling on the outside yet peaceful on the inside, just as it is possible (and all too common) to sit still in "prayer" while the mind races and plots. If Mary had been sitting at Jesus' feet and thinking, *Why doesn't He tell my sister to slow down?* then she would have received the rebuke.

Obviously the sisters' relationship with their Lord was natural enough to allow for plenty of give-and-take. They loved and worshiped Him, but they also felt free to speak their minds to Him, as they both did when they said, "If you had been here, [our] brother would not have died" (John 11:21,32). My hunch is that these people, more than anyone else, including His own relatives, were Jesus' family. Here was His home away from home. We might say that for Him this humble household in Bethany was the closest He came to heaven on earth.

On the road, another person who provided such friendship for Jesus was John, "the disciple Jesus loved." Does God really love some people more than others? No, "God does not show favoritism" (Romans 2:11). Yet somehow even He needs a best friend. John, literally a bosom buddy, could with perfect naturalness lean upon Jesus' breast at the Last Supper. He was the disciple with whom Jesus was able to be most Himself.

How vital it is for those in the public eye to have friends with whom they can relax and be at home. Anyone who can be a safe, guileless friend to a person in power is providing an extraordinary service. Since all of us, in our own conceited little ways, are people of power, anyone who humbly befriends us is bestowing the greatest of gifts. Religious people have a tendency to be spiritually intense. If we are spiritually intense ourselves, it is no good being surrounded with others who are equally intense. Perhaps this is one reason why Jesus spent little time with John the Baptist, while He did go frequently to the home of Lazarus.

As human beings we were not made to relate on an entirely spiritual plane. Overspiritualization is a strong temptation that has led many astray. Friendship is the mitigator of this unholy excess. As candlelight, in contrast to the glare of electricity, lends a room a soft glow, so friendship softens and naturalizes our religious zeal. As Jesus is the mediator of our relationship with the Father, so friends can mediate our relationship with Jesus. Jesus brings us to God, but friends can bring us to Jesus. How many of us have been in the position of the paralytic who had to be brought to Jesus by his friends (see Mark 2)? As Jesus is the key to the heart of the Father, so friends offer the key to the heart of Jesus.

Jesus Himself did not accomplish what He did alone. He chose to work with friends. What did Jesus' friends do for Him? I believe they helped Him (as heretical as this may sound) to be more human. After all, humanity was something Jesus learned about as He went along, just as we all do. This is a service we too can perform for God: We can humanize Him! We talk of "ministering to the Lord," but do we believe it? Do we really believe we have something to give Him? By being as human as possible, we provide a home for the King of the universe, a resting place for His mercy. Isn't this what our King wants: to be at home on earth as He is in heaven?

CHAPTER 61

Cliques

When Jesus was choosing His disciples, He must have been aware of the danger of forming a clique. That is why He did not choose only from among His own intimate friends, but rather settled on a much more diverse team that included a despised tax collector, a left-wing radical, and even a man He knew would betray Him to death. This was no mutual admiration society but a cross section of society itself.

No wonder Jesus spent an entire night in prayer before selecting this group. Doubtless He knew already who His own closest friends were; to choose them would have been easy. But Jesus was seeking not His own will but His Father's. What friends would His Father choose for Him? Even when it came to those who would sit at His right and His left in glory, Jesus said these places were not for Him but for His Father to assign (Matthew 20:23).

Who are your friends? Have you chosen them carefully, or are they people you have gravitated to out of laziness? Have you let God choose your friends for you? Besides His motley crew of disciples, Jesus had many other unlikely friends, including beggars, prostitutes, lepers, and the hated Samaritans. Can you count among your friends a homeless or disabled person, a prisoner, a homosexual, or someone of a different race or faith?

Or what about the stranger? Is the stranger your friend—the one you pass in the street, the one who sits beside you on the bus, the one behind you in the lineup at the government office? What is your attitude to these unknown people? Do you regard them with indifference and cold suspicion or with a welcoming warmth? How friendly are you? To the extent that you do not welcome the stranger, you will be a stranger to yourself. Try viewing the stranger as a friend you haven't met, and you may find yourself entertaining angels or the Lord Himself.

It is nice to be surrounded by people with whom one feels comfortable and accepted. But my world must be larger than that. Once I know what true friendship is and have some real friends, I must take that gift and extend it to others. That is, I need to rub shoulders with people who make me uncomfortable, and learn to be comfortable with them too. Inherent in friendship is the desire to befriend others. Without this outward-looking energy, any circle of friends will gradually deteriorate and collapse.

The range and depth of your friendships accurately reflects your knowledge of the love of God. Paul prayed for the Ephesians that they might "grasp how wide and long and high and deep is the love of Christ" (3:18). The best way to do this is to know and love a wide and varied group of people. God's love is wide because it embraces all of humanity. It is long because it extends throughout entire lifetimes and on into eternity. God's love is high because it comes from heaven. And it is deep because it saves, reaching to the very bottom of the hell in our hearts.

Our circle of friends should be like God Himself—much too large and mysterious for us to comprehend, control, or pigeonhole. Our friendships should not merely reinforce our present values but also challenge them. How thankful I am to have friends whose views on politics, sex, and religion differ markedly from mine. Such people enlarge my capacity to love. Though I do not agree with them on many issues, I know that the basis of understanding is not rational agreement but love.

The truth of this last statement is easily demonstrated. For where there is a high degree of moral and theological agreement, love may still be absent and schisms erupt. In fact, the more we limit our friendships to those who think as we do, the more the slightest differences in thinking will threaten our unity.

When I became a Christian, I opened my heart to Jesus. At the time I was a long way from having a correct theology. But correct theology wasn't necessary for forming a relationship with Jesus. Indeed good theology often gets in the way of enjoying friendship with God. Similarly with people, thinking the same way is not fundamentally what relationship is about.

Therefore our friendships must be rooted not in conformity but in love. Cultural and philosophical differences form a rich soil in which love may flourish. Often stridently held opinions are merely a mask to protect the vulnerable person inside. This real, inner person is the one who needs befriending. The uglier the exterior, the greater the need for someone to see and love the tender soul within.

We cannot practice the presence of one person without practicing the presence of all. Until we love our enemies we cannot properly love our friends. The one person with whom we are angry will cast a shadow over the one we love best. Loving people is like eating peanuts: One leads to another and another and another. To see God's image in one is to see Him in all. Before you know it, all your petty judgments and prejudices will collapse around you like a house of cards, leaving love alone, the King of hearts, still standing.

CHAPTER 62

Fear of Man

*T*he greatest enemy of friendship is fear. *Fear of man,* as it's sometimes called, is a form of idolatry. It's proof that people are
being put in the place of God. Such fear may not always feel like fear,
but it tends to manifest itself in one of two ways: either in the dom-
ination and control of others, or else in the need to impress people,
standing in their shadow and letting them pull our strings. Either
way the result is not friendship but alienation.

Alienation stems from always putting ourselves either higher or
lower than others, never on the same level. But friends regard one
another as equals. Wherever there is an idol, there is a pedestal.
Either we place ourselves on the pedestal, or we place others there.
Often two people will trade the pedestal back and forth, each one
using their strength to exploit the other's weakness. In modern par-
lance this is known as a *codependent relationship.* Pedestal-traders are
more concerned with power and position than with love. They will
settle for being exploited so long as they in turn can exploit. Feeling
that they are never quite good enough, what else can they do but
scorn, judge, and belittle others?

Fear is the inappropriate surrender of our power. There is only One to whom we are to give power, and hence the song of heaven goes, "To him who sits on the throne and to the Lamb be praise and honor and glory and power" (Revelation 5:13). If we're letting people control us—or (which amounts to the same) trying to control them—then those people are our gods. It does not matter what we believe theologically. If the person beside us is pulling our strings, then that person is, at that moment, functionally our god.

How daring the Lord was to create Eve! What if the man started listening to her more than to Him? What if he found her presence more alluring than the presence of God and feared her opinion more than His? Of course, this is exactly what happened, and the rest is history. People set other people in the place of God. It is possible to idolize anyone, including spouse, friends, pastors, even children.

An idol is a false god who controls us, but only because we have set out to control it. Idolizing people is the opposite of practicing their presence. If we fail to see the image of God in others, we are bound to see an image of our own making. We'll see a phantom, a ghost, someone who is not really there. When we devalue others in this way, the result is that we ourselves feel cheapened and unloved.

If only we would surrender all desire for control, then we could no longer be controlled. The surrender of control is not done passively but through radical action. The phoniness in relationships must be deliberately broken—for example, by telling the truth, confessing sins, learning to say no, or speaking words of blessing. Such steps are never easy, but they are always liberating. Idols by their nature feel stiff, wooden, contrived. How refreshing to smash these artificial relationships and enter into living friendships!

Friendship involves systematically weeding out all false ways of relating and choosing the one way of love. Didn't Jesus always know exactly what to do? Our friends are those who somehow manage to have just the right word for us, the right gesture, the right touch—who possess the secret of continually breaking through our artificiality and restoring us to humanity.

"Narrow [is] the road that leads to life" (Matthew 7:14)—as narrow as the one person you are with, as narrow as doing the one thing necessary to grow closer to that person. Many people feel trapped in their lives and cannot see the way out. They wish they were somewhere else, doing something else, with different people. They wish they had made other choices, and they think, *If only I knew how to get myself out of my present situation, then I could begin to live.*

The problem is, the only way to get from here to there is by starting here. Life cannot begin somewhere else or in the future but only right here and now. Do not wait to be free before you can be free. Be free now. All those who have attained freedom have attained it in their immediate circumstances—whether behind bars, in difficult job situations, or in troubled relationships.

This is what Jesus meant when He said, "Be faithful in small things." The small things are the ordinary circumstances in which you find yourself—especially your present relationships. Be faithful and courageous in this arena, and gradually a larger life will open up to you.

CHAPTER 63

People from Porlock

Samuel Taylor Coleridge's poem "Kubla Khan" has a fascinating story attached to it. It seems this poem came to Coleridge full blown in a dream. Upon awaking, still in a kind of trance, he immediately wrote down the first fifty-four lines. Then a knock came at the door, and for over an hour his writing was interrupted by a visitor from the nearby village of Porlock. By the time the poet returned to work, his strange state of illumination had passed. After that he was never able to finish his poem.

The visitor from Porlock, though nameless, has become a famous man. Generations of poetry lovers and scholars have taken their turn in reviling this uncouth visitor for his role in ruining Coleridge's masterpiece.

But think: Without this man from Porlock, what would we have? Just one more great and inspired poem. With him, however, we have one of the most intriguing anecdotes in literary history. As it stands, there is enough of Coleridge's poem to give a good idea of the whole. The story of the man from Porlock only adds to it. And what it adds, to my mind, is more interesting than the completed poem would have been.

As a writer, I too get interrupted in moments of high inspiration. Even as a human being, I often seem to be surrounded by people from Porlock. Why don't they leave me alone and visit me only when it's convenient?

Years ago someone asked me about the greatest desire of my life. I replied, "I want to live all alone on an island and have people come to me to learn about God." Recalling these words now, I shudder. Though at the time it seemed such a noble goal, I see now the perversity of it. I was seeking not love but power.

Perhaps all of us, in one way or another in every relationship, nurse a secret desire to be the one who holds the power. Isn't this what keeps us from forming healthy friendships? No one can enter the house of friendship without checking all pride and pretense at the door. Friendship is the great leveler, the destroyer of isolation. No man is an island, but we all take a stab at living on one and trying to get others to come to us and bow down.

Gradually I'm learning that the intruders in my life are no accident. In fact they may well be sent by God, not to interrupt my writing or my solitude, but to make my life more interesting. It may even turn out that the Porlockians are angels in disguise. Where I fear inconvenience, God intends enrichment. Where I see a complication, God sees a glorious mystery. Isn't this what people are for—to make our lives more interesting than any poem, more inspiring than inspiration itself?

Coleridge's poem portrays a vision of paradise, complete with a fabulous "pleasure dome," a "sacred river," and "gardens bright with sinuous rills." It seems to me that the visitor from Porlock was not an interruption in this inspired vision but a part of it. Perhaps he was a messenger from God sent to remind Coleridge (and all of us) that no one can inhabit paradise alone. Porlock is an essential place in paradise, for the greatest pleasure lies not in vision or in poetry but in human community.

CHAPTER 64

The Glass Slipper

I'll never forget the ending of Federico Fellini's film *8 ½*. I saw the movie only once, long ago, and at the time I didn't understand it. It all seemed like a dream, which I'm sure was exactly the director's intent. But at some level I gathered it was an autobiographical portrayal of Fellini's own search for identity—or perhaps *belonging* is a better word.

The film is about its own making, about a director in search of a script. Already a set is under construction, a cast is being hired, all the wheels of the film industry are rolling—but what exactly is this film about? What is the story? The director, whose name is Guido, doesn't know. He feels confused and frightened. He wants to tell a story about himself, but because his life is not coming together in reality, neither will it come together in art.

Guido's assembled cast includes professional actors, but it also includes ordinary people—in fact all the people who happen to be a part of his life. The entire film is composed of fragmentary scenes showing Guido in various encounters with the grotesque-seeming cast of his own life. In some ways he appears to be the one "normal" person in a crowd of aliens. Yet it is all too obvious that he, too, is lonely and estranged, involved with these people but not connected to them, cut off not only from others but from himself.

Guido cannot make a film about himself because he cannot accept his life as it is. Especially he cannot accept that he himself is no better or different than the relationships he has formed. The sum and meaning of his life is not to be found in art, but in people. The people he knows—all of them—these *are* his life. Can the great director, who is so good at bringing actors together to make great films, succeed in bringing together real people to make a great life?

Not until the end does Guido emerge from his limbo of alienation to join hands, literally, with his cast. There they are, all the unlikely souls of his acquaintance, dancing in a circle. Finally Guido leaves his lonely position in the center and joins the circle dance. No longer aloof, he is connected, a part of his own show, one with his people. This scene has haunted me for some twenty years.

The title of this film, *8 ½*, refers both to the number of Fellini's films and also to his shoe size. At the end Guido steps into his proper place, the shoe that fits him. That place is the circle of people with whom he happens to have shared his life. For he realizes that he doesn't just "happen" to be with this odd assortment of characters. No, these are the people he himself has chosen to associate with, just as he has chosen the cast for his films. These are *his* people. Ultimately Guido's choice of all the people he knows becomes conscious, deliberate, owned. Rather than remaining estranged from his own life, he puts it on like a comfortable pair of shoes. And when he does—behold, like a glass slipper in a fairy tale, it fits!

Have you put on your life? Do you wear it comfortably? Or does this one mysterious life of yours, the only life you have, chafe and irritate you like an ill-fitting pair of shoes? Consider the circle of people with whom you intermingle—whether past or present, close or distant, small or great. Have you joined these people? Have you accepted them as your own? Do they belong to you, and you to them? Or are you lurking outside the circle, wishing you belonged to some different group?

If your relationships are unhealthy, it may be that you need to ditch your current friends and get a new batch. But at some point you must face the necessity of accepting the people who are actually a part of you. Those whom God has already chosen for you, you must choose for yourself. Somehow you must join hands with all those unlikely monsters and dance the dance of friendship. What are you waiting for? If you're lurking outside the circle, it is not because you are different, but because you are proud. Come down from your lonely tower and join the dance!

The circle is waiting for you. You are the only one missing. You are the only one who can close this circle and make it complete, and so bring your heart the wholeness it craves. No one else can do this for you. No one else can draw together this particular circle. No one else can fill this gap. This is your place. These are your people. No one else can know them for you. Will you look around at these faces in your circle—these tender, bright flowers of flesh patiently uplifted in hope of love—and will you own them as your own? Will you know them and be known?

This, finally, is who you are. Here lies the secret of your identity. Peering into these faces, you will recognize yourself. You will know yourself.

In the end, who you are is who you know.

CHAPTER 65

The Day I
Married People

*I*n 1985 I published a book entitled *The Mystery of Marriage*. It
could easily have been called *A Funny Thing Happened on the
Way to the Monastery*. It tells the story of a would-be monk who
stumbles into marriage and discovers, in the excruciating wine press
of married love, that there is no spirituality more exacting, no Christian discipline more profound, no monastic life more glorious and
liberating than the arms of a wife.

Little did I realize that years later I would arrive at a similar conclusion regarding the entire human race.

One Sunday morning I happened to attend an evangelistic service. Toward the end the minister issued an altar call, inviting those
to come forward who wished to give their lives to Jesus. I was already
a Christian and felt no need of making a fresh commitment. However, as the song "Just As I Am" began to play, I felt another kind of
stirring in my soul.

It was a feeling, I think, similar to what was going on inside those few others who even now were making their way up to the altar. In those moments my heart was strangely warmed. Deep emotion was rising in me, yet at the same time I was aware of an interior struggle taking place. I knew that I had something important but difficult to do.

Inside me a light was dawning, and it took the form of this strange thought: *While I knew I had given myself to Jesus, I knew also that I had never really given myself to people.* Something in me had always held back, guarded, insecure, stilted, untrusting. Whereas Jesus seemed approachable because He offered unconditional love, people were a mixed bag. In many ways I had learned to let go and let God, but with people I could never quite let myself go. Accordingly, while my faith was ever so spiritual, I was lacking in simple human warmth.

Years before I had come close to entering a monastery, only to fall in love and get married instead. But marriage, too, to my great surprise, had turned into a rather comfy sort of monastery, a place where I could hide from my sense of social inadequacy. Now I felt the Lord calling me to come out of my monk's cell, to walk forward into the arms of my inadequacy, and to give myself to people. Moreover, it was time to stand up and make a public commitment to this effect, just as I had stood at the altar with Karen and publicly exchanged wedding vows.

So I answered this call. That day, along with all those who went forward to give their lives to Jesus, I rose before the assembly and gave myself to the people. I actually stood up and said, "I love you all, and I want to marry you."

For me this was a tremendous and mysterious step. I could not know all that it meant, nor did I feel any special strength to carry it out. But I'd been running from people all my life, and it was time to turn around and walk the other way. Having invited Jesus into my heart, it was time now to invite people in. For the conviction had overwhelmed me that this is what it means to be a Christian.

As I took this step, I felt changed. A certain struggle would continue to play itself out in my social life, just as it had in the early years of my marriage. But I knew now that I had embarked upon a new course. I had moved in and set up housekeeping with the human race. For better or worse, for richer or poorer, in sickness and in health, I was home now. At home with people.

Epilogue

Here is a parable the Lord told to my friend Chris Walton. Imagine you are traveling from point A to point B. After many struggles, eventually you make it to point B, but as you look back you realize you have left a trail of damaged relationships: people you have ignored, belittled, hurt, or even stepped on in order to attain your goal.

Now imagine, again, that you are traveling from point A to point B. But this time you seek peace in all your relationships. You take notice of those people you formerly overlooked. You go out of your way to help and to honor others. In the process of doing all this, however, you never make it to point B.

After presenting these two scenarios, the Lord asked Chris, "Which way would you rather travel?"

"The second way," admitted Chris.

"You see?" said the Lord. "I measure success differently."

While collecting material for a book on visions of heaven, I heard the following anonymous story:

⟶

I found myself before the gates of heaven. The gates were not pearly but golden, and it was not Peter who stood there but Jesus.

The Lord stood right in the doorway as a long line of people filed before Him. On His left appeared another opening, which I saw to be a one-way escalator going down and down, disappearing into blackness. Most of those waiting to see Jesus did not get a chance to talk to Him, for when their turn came, He simply pointed them toward the mouth of the escalator, and down they went. It was perfectly obvious where they were going. As for the others, He beckoned each one in turn to come and stand before Him, as He asked this one simple question:

"Did you learn how to love?"

The people answered this question in many different ways, each according to his character. But their words did not matter; in every case it was clear that the answer could be reduced to a simple yes or no. There were no gray areas here. Either the people had learned how to love, or they hadn't. Obviously these were all Christians. They had not been sent down the escalator. Yet some had learned how to love and some had not. Most, in fact, had not.

So Jesus kept asking His probing little question, and the answers came back: "Well, not really"; "I'm not quite sure"; "I did my best, Lord"; and so on. Whenever a negative response was either stated or implied, the Lord showed no sign of displeasure. His face was all love, all compassion. It seemed He wished only for each person to say the words aloud, to admit the truth for themselves. Then, with a gesture of lavish munificence, He stood aside to wave that person through the gates into heaven. And in they went to their eternal reward.

Most interesting of all were those few souls who were able to answer the Lord's question in the affirmative. Their answers too took many forms, yet each stood out as more colorful and inspired than the negative answers had been.

"Wow, Lord!" cried one person. "Did I *ever* learn how to love!"

"Love, love, love!" chanted another. "What a gas!"

These people's faces were not just radiant but explosive with joy. Some who spoke most quietly had the brightest faces of all. None of these people exhibited any doubt or uncertainty. All those who had truly learned how to love knew it.

Moreover, to my great astonishment, these people entered into heaven through a different gate than the others had. For whenever a true lover stood before the Lord, He opened His arms wide to receive them. This was no ordinary hug, for in the midst of it the Lord's breast opened up, and the people who had learned how to love passed into heaven right through the center of His heart!

Each time this happened I gasped in wonder. It was so beautiful! I knew that right here was the central mystery of life, and to see it melted my own heart in purest bliss. The ecstasy was fleeting, however, for it often happened that the next person in line was sent down the escalator. And so the wonderful secret would close up again.

Yet I've never forgotten it. One scene, especially, I have replayed in my memory countless times. I saw a black woman approach the heavenly gates surrounded by a great entourage of angels. Instinctively I knew that these were all the ministering spirits who had attended this woman during her lifetime. When a heart is full of love, angels are free to minister to that person. Most people bind their angels with loads of resentment and hate. But whenever someone sincerely chooses to forgive and to love, ministering spirits are released to accompany that soul throughout its life's journey. You can imagine what a tremendous benefit it is to have angels always close at hand, whispering the truth in one's ear, warning of danger, lending every sort of help.

This black woman in my vision had so many angels accompanying her that she looked like the grand finale of a Broadway musical. No solemn procession this, but the whole company came before the Lord singing and dancing for all they were worth, with the woman in the lead conducting and cheering them on like a majorette. I wish I could remember the words of her song, but I cannot; it may have been too holy for my ears to comprehend. But the look on her face! Oh—she was indescribably jubilant, utterly intoxicated with love! Drawing near to Jesus, she missed not a beat of her gala parade, for the Lord did not stop her for one moment—not even to ask her the great question—but rather His heart immediately opened up and the whole joyous throng went waltzing through into eternal splendor.

Now that's what I call traveling in style!

⌒⌒⌒⌒

I once heard a famous preacher, in the midst of a sermon to five thousand people, pause to say, "I love this. I really love this. I just came from a holiday with my wife, and that was pretty nice. We had a good time together. But it wasn't as good as this. There's nothing better than this."

That preacher was wrong. He was out of touch with what's really important. He was a workaholic. Oh, he delivered a great sermon. One could feel the presence of God powerfully as he spoke. And in the time of ministry that followed, miracles happened.

Still, when this man paused to comment on his marriage, what he might have said was, "I wish I had the guts to love my wife the way I love my work. I wish I could love my family and friends this way too. Matter of fact, I wish I could love, period." This statement would have been honest.

The church is dying for lack of love. The world is dying for lack of church. There are too many pastors who love their work more than they love people. There are too many Christians who love their religion but do not love themselves. Far from "living a life of love," weeks pass us by with barely an intimate moment. In churches, in families, in neighborhoods, entire relationships are lived out with hardly a point of real connection.

Meanwhile, it's a day in December and I'm walking beside the ocean with my wife, Karen. The sun, that awesome, pendant globe of fire, is shining so gloriously that I suddenly remember it is really a star, a star so close and bright that it banishes all darkness. The radiant sea, the golden sand, the pure white wheeling gulls—this whole scene is like something we have never seen before, as if we were on some other planet, in some other galaxy. As if we were in heaven.

But no, we are right here on earth, and we are together, just the two of us. This being at my side is no angel but my wife. If she were an angel she would be less strange to me, less dazzling, less beautiful. It is impossible to capture in words the wonder of just being with her.

If it were nothing more than her hair, the soft dark splendor of it, and the way the wind lifts it in wisps to lay across her cheek with perfect deft-fingered grace, and how all the colors in the world and more limn each strand like shining beads of dew—if the glory of Karen were nothing more than this, it would be enough. It would be too much; I would be more than satisfied.

But these few strands of hair are just a tiny part of Karen. She is so much more than this, so much that is both visible and invisible, both lucid and ineffable. The magic of her presence is like electricity running lightly and thrillingly all through my body and soul. I'm not just aware of her; she's a part of me. I'm practicing her presence. Or is her presence practicing me? Whatever's happening, it is completely intoxicating, completely pure.

Though we talk a little, I'm not thinking about what we're saying. It's our mouths, our eyes, our hands that carry the meaning, while our words are like physical things, like beautiful stones we pick up and pass between us. We fall silent for long stretches. There's not the least pressure to say anything or not to, to do anything except be who we are.

Laughter comes easily, and other moods too flow through us like wind touching water. There is utter freedom to feel everything. So precious is this that tears keep welling up in me. It's not just that tears come to my eyes, but as if tears are oozing from all the pores in my face, giving it a sheen of splendor. I can feel myself glowing, burning, and the same fire is on Karen too. It's the glory of God. The engine of grace is grinding golden flour out of every cell in our bodies. Clean, holy fire is sweeping through us, touching us all over like loving fingers, like warm flakes of gently falling golden snow...

Words fail. All I know is that I'm standing on holy ground. All I know is that my heart burns within me, as surely as it did for the two disciples who walked beside a stranger on the road to Emmaus. I'm reminded of a line from the musical *Les Misérables:* "To love another person is to see the face of God." God is love, so to be with Karen like this, to be with anyone like this, is to keep company with God.

I'm not saying that Karen and I live in this exalted state all the time. But it does happen a lot. And it also happens with a wider and wider circle of people. In my family, in my church, in all my relationships I experience more and more of this quiet, lovely miracle. It's called love, and as Christians we're expected to have more and more of it, until finally we live it and breathe it.

There's nothing better than this. As far as I'm concerned, this is it. If there's more, then this is the foundation for everything else. As Paul put it so plainly, "If I have a faith that can move mountains, but have not love, I am nothing" (1 Corinthians 13:2). He might have gone on to say, "If I make a phone call, attend a meeting, or go to the corner store for a loaf of bread, but do it without love, I gain nothing."

Nothing is simpler, nothing is more exalted, nothing is more powerful than this ordinary glory of love that comes from practicing the presence of God and of people. This is really all I want out of life anymore. With this in place, my life is full. To paraphrase David in Psalm 23, "The LORD is my shepherd, and there's nothing more I want."

Notes

People

1. Jim Harrison, *Just Before Dark: Collected Nonfiction* (Livingstone, Mont.: Clark City Press, 1991).

2. From an interview with Carol Shields on *Writers and Company* (CBC Radio, March 1998).

3. Stephen Lawhead, *The Paradise War* (Oxford: Lion Publishing, 1991), 413.

4. Brother Lawrence of the Resurrection, *The Practice of the Presence of God*, trans. John J. Delaney (Garden City, N.Y.: Image Books, 1977), 43.

Self

1. Brother Lawrence, *The Practice of the Presence of God*, 40.

2. Brother Lawrence, *The Practice of the Presence of God*, 57.

3. Annie Dillard, "Notes for Young Writers," *Image*, no. 16 (Summer 1997): 66-7.

4. Brother Lawrence, *The Practice of the Presence of God*, 90.

5. Brother Lawrence, *The Practice of the Presence of God,* 92.

6. Brother Lawrence, *The Practice of the Presence of God,* 85.

7. Brother Lawrence, *The Practice of the Presence of God,* 89.

8. Brother Lawrence, *The Practice of the Presence of God,* 47.

9. Brother Lawrence, *The Practice of the Presence of God,* 47.

10. Marianne Williamson, *A Return to Love* (New York: HarperCollins, 1993), 188-9.

PRESENCE

1. Brother Lawrence, *The Practice of the Presence of God,* 38-9.

2. Agnes Sanford, *The Healing Light* (New York: Walker, 1986).

3. Raymond Carver, *Where I'm Calling From: New and Selected Stories* (New York: Atlantic Monthly Press, 1988), 279.

PRACTICE

1. Brother Lawrence, *The Practice of the Presence of God,* 87-8.

2. Brother Lawrence, *The Practice of the Presence of God,* 109.

3. Brother Lawrence, *The Practice of the Presence of God,* 62.

4. Brother Lawrence, *The Practice of the Presence of God,* 40.

5. Brother Lawrence, *The Practice of the Presence of God*, 68.

6. Brother Lawrence, *The Practice of the Presence of God*, 42.

7. Julia A. Fletcher, "Little Things," 1845.

8. Brother Lawrence, *The Practice of the Presence of God*, 42.

9. Brother Lawrence, *The Practice of the Presence of God*, 57.

10. Brother Lawrence, *The Practice of the Presence of God*, 99.

11. Brother Lawrence, *The Practice of the Presence of God*, 49.

FRIENDSHIP

1. George MacDonald quoted in Michael R. Phillips, *George MacDonald: Scotland's Beloved Storyteller* (Minneapolis, Minn.: Bethany, 1987).

2. Frederick Buechner, *Godric* (San Francisco: Harper & Row, 1980), 7.